Intimate Instructions
in
Integer Basic

Dr. George H. Blackwood is a retired Navy pilot and a former college professor with bachelor's, master's, education specialist, and doctor of philosophy degrees. He now devotes full time to writing.

Brian D. Blackwood has studied computer science and engineering at Michigan State University. For the last four years he has been employed as a supervisor at a large data processing center that services banks and financial institutions.

Intimate Instructions
in
Integer Basic

by

Brian D. Blackwood
George H. Blackwood

Howard W. Sams & Co., Inc.
4300 WEST 62ND ST. INDIANAPOLIS, INDIANA 46268 USA

International Standard Book Number: 0-672-21812-7
Library of Congress Card Number: 81-51551

Edited by: *Frank N. Speights*
Illustrated by: *Wm. D. Basham*

Printed in the United States of America.

Preface

This book is written for people who need the most basic view of BASIC and who do not have a computer specialist available when they need help. This book is coauthored by two people. One is a person who has very little understanding of computers and computer programming, and the other is a person who is an expert in the field. This book is written on a level that is overly simplistic in order to try to give some technical information to people who buy a computer and who are then stumped as to what to do after the two-position power switch is turned "on." This book is planned so the most nontechnical person will be able to write and utilize simple programs, and will also be able to understand and modify more complicated programs.

For a middle-aged, nonmathematical, noncomputer-oriented person, the computer was to be a link between the generations. The mystery of "computing" and the computer was compounded by listening to a son who is a computer engineer. The magazine advertisements I read factually stated that young children could learn to program games and simulation processes before they had completed the BASIC Programming Manual. The thought of having all that power was euphoric.

An Apple II with 48K of RAM memory was purchased in November, 1978. The salesman gave some mystical incantations, demonstrated how to turn the thing on, punched some buttons, and lo, a game came on the screen. He recorded some programs on a cassette tape, inspected the machine to see that it was working properly, and sent me on my way to become a computer programmer overnight. This did not happen. Several months later, the ability to program was still not apparent. The thought of destroying the "exacting" computer crossed my mind more than once. If my son, the computer engineer, had not been available for consultation, my feeble efforts at programming would have been terminated. With his help, the struggle goes on slowly, very slowly.

Remember that for programs to RUN, the computer will accept only perfection. The change of a comma or semicolon makes a difference in the formatting and in the meaning of a program. It also makes a difference as to whether the program will run or not. In writing this book, an explanation of these technical details that are so necessary to computer programming is attempted.

This programming book is specifically written for the Apple II microcomputer that uses Integer BASIC language, but it is applicable, with modifications, to any computer using BASIC language.

GEORGE H. BLACKWOOD

Contents

Introduction

This book is written at the lowest possible level. It is assumed that you, the reader, have no knowledge of programming and only a desire to learn. Many times in typing the manuscript, I said to myself, "I am repeating the same information over and over." Thus, many times the same information is repeated, but from a slightly different aspect. Semantic understanding varies from person to person. If the repetitious aspect is boring, my apologies to you, but if it enhances learning and understanding, its purpose has been accomplished.

Programming is detailed, exacting, and thought provoking. Do not expect to become an expert programmer overnight. As with anything worthwhile, it will take effort on your part to comprehend this new medium. Misleading advertising makes the public believe that anyone can program. An ad reads that a thirteen-year-old boy has not even completed the programming manual, yet he has just programmed the Space Wars game. Don't you believe it!

In programming, every symbol, character, comma, semicolon, and colon means something to the machine and you have to know "what" they mean to the machine. This is no comic book—everything in it means something specific. Read it as if your programming ability depended on every word. Read it and digest it.

Programming is the truest form of building on a foundation. Each stone builds on the previous stone. If you do not understand what is in Lesson 1, don't go to Lesson 2. Each rule must be understood not only for itself, but also how it relates to rules around it. The microcomputer must be told exactly what to do and in what sequence to do it. The microcomputer knows nothing and assumes nothing. You must be smarter than the machine to make the machine react properly. The information in each lesson must be thoroughly understood, practiced, and retained before moving to the next lesson. As the cliche goes, "Hardware is soft, but software is hard."

As you learn the rules of programming (software), experiment with the rules and make changes in the program statements to determine what effect these changes will have on the program. Reinforce your learning experience in any way that is best for you.

Do not force the learning experience. It only causes frustration and decreases learning ability. If you are a morning (diurnal) person, set your study time in the morning. If you are a nocturnal person, set your study time in the evening. Study in a time and environment that is most receptive to your learning.

After you have learned the rules, you must practice, practice, practice. If you don't use your new ability, you will lose it.

Unless a computer has a hardware problem, it does not make mistakes. Many times you have heard the statement made about a mistake on a bill—"It's the computer's fault." Don't you believe it! The problem is with either the program or the input. If a mistake comes from a computer, it is probably a "people" mistake, and you must have people correct the mistake.

Computers are a great part of our daily lives and they will be a greater part of our future. The more you understand about microcomputer operations and programming, the better understanding you will have of the future. Computers, per se, will not replace petroleum products, but they may affect your future as they help to overcome the present shortages of petroleum. Fig. 1 is a view of the Apple II microcomputer.

Most of all, if this is your hobby, enjoy it both as a method of relaxation and as a stress breaker. The computer is one thing you can completely control. It doesn't go into a sand trap, like the golf ball, or talk back to you, like your spouse or kids. While it must be told exactly what to do, you can learn to do it in a relaxed and enjoyable style. Have fun and enjoy the book.

Fig. 1-1. The Apple II microcomputer.

LESSON 1

Clear the VDM Screen

To begin operation, turn the off-on switch on the Apple II computer to the "on" position. The switch is located at the back of the computer on the left-hand side. Now switch the tv set to the "on" position. Hereafter, the tv set will be referred to either as the video display module (VDM) or as the screen. The power light on the keyboard of the computer lights up and the screen also lights up. For convenience sake, the keyboard of the Apple II is shown in Fig. 1-1. Pictures and descriptions of the keys (control, escape, and reset) can be found on pages 6 to 16 in *Apple II Basic Programming Manual*.

Now, clear the video display module screen by following the sequence given below:

1. Press the RESET key and then release it.
2. Press the control (CTRL) key and the B key simultaneously and, then, release them.
3. Press the RETURN key and release it.
4. Press the escape (ESC) key and release it.
5. Press both the SHIFT and P keys simultaneously and, then, release them.
6. Press the RETURN key and release it.

The video display module should now be clear with only the blinking cursor showing in the upper left-hand corner of the screen. The VDM is now prepared to receive input that is typed in from the keyboard. Important: *It is essential that the return key be pressed after each completed operation* or the computer will not function.

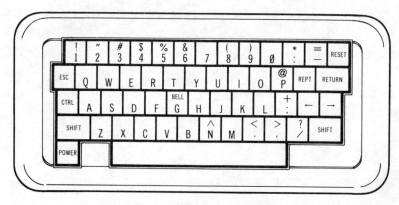

Fig. 1-1. The Apple keyboard.

The cursor is controlled by the left pointing (shift left) and right pointing (shift right) arrow keys. Type in the numbers 1, 2, and 3. To erase a number (or numbers) move the cursor to the left by pressing the shift left key until the cursor is over a specific number. If the cursor is moved to cover number 3, and RETURN is pressed, number 3 is erased and numbers 1 and 2 are printed on the screen. The cursor is shifted one line down (actually, the 1 and 2 scroll up) and a clear line is ready for more input. Now, type ASD. The cursor rests after the D. Press the shift left key and move the cursor to cover the D. When RETURN is pressed, the D is erased, but the computer beeps, prints AS and *** SYNTAX ERR. The screen now shows:

```
>12              (12 are called numeric characters)
>AS              (AS are called alpha characters)
*** SYNTAX ERR
>■
```

(12AS is called an alphanumeric character string.)

The syntax error message indicates that the computer does not accept alpha (alphabetical) information in this form. In programming, all program statements must start with a line number, from 0 (zero) to 32767, usually in increments of 10. The following example shows why 32767 is the maximum number that can be used. Type in this program.

```
10      LET A = 2      press RETURN
20      LET B = 3      press RETURN
32768   END            press RETURN
*** > 32767  ERR
```

The integer 32768 will not be accepted by the microcomputer. Any number in excess of −32767 or +32767 will cause the computer to print *** > 32767 ERR because the Apple II microcomputer, using Integer BASIC, is designed not to accept numbers outside the range of −32767 and +32767.

Now, type LIST and press the RETURN key. LIST causes the program statements (or program), which have been properly typed, to appear on the screen.

There is a shorter routine that prepares the microcomputer for programming, but it does not clear the video module screen. After the VDM and the microcomputer are turned "on," use the following routine:

1. Press the RESET key and then release it.
2. Press the control (CTRL) key and the B key simultaneously and, then, release them.
3. Press the RETURN key and then release it.

If the RESET key is accidentally pressed during computer operations, a machine language code will appear on the screen. To gain operational control of the microcomputer and cause a return to Integer BASIC, press the control (CTRL) and C keys together. (Hereafter, the CTRL key will be written as CONTROL for clarification. In addition, when two keys are to be pressed simultaneously, they will be shown with three dashes separating them, as follows: CONTROL---C.) The letter C should not be printed on the screen. If the letter C is printed on the screen, the C key was pressed before the CONTROL key. Note that CONTROL---C does not erase the computer memory. However, CONTROL---B will erase the computer memory. Another way to clear the computer memory is to type NEW and press the RETURN key. To check to see if the computer memory has been cleared, type LIST and press the RETURN key. If nothing shows on the screen, memory is clear.

To clear memory:

1. Press CONTROL---B and press RETURN.
2. Type NEW and press RETURN.

To check to see that memory is clear (after the NEW—RETURN entry):

1. Type LIST and then press RETURN. (If nothing appears on the screen, the memory is clear.)

Type in lines 10 and 20 of the previous program and LIST the program. Now, press CONTROL---C, press RETURN, and release. The cursor returns to the screen. Type LIST and press RETURN. The program returns to the screen. Now, press RESET, press CONTROL---B, release, and, then, press RETURN. Now, type LIST and press RETURN. Voila, no program.

LESSON 2

Load and Save Program

After completion of this lesson, you should be able to:

1. Load a program into memory.
2. Save a program stored in memory.

VOCABULARY

Library—a collection of proven or standard routines, or parts of routines, contained in storage and available for problem-solving processes either with or without further modification.

Line number—the positive integer that each program statement begins with.

LIST—causes a program to be displayed on the screen.

LOAD—reads (LOADs) the BASIC program from cassette tape into memory.

NEW—clears the current BASIC program from memory.

Output—results produced by the microcomputer.

Program statement—an instruction to the microcomputer that is stored in memory.

RUN—the performance of one program or routine.

PROGRAM EXAMPLE

Programs that are typed on the keyboard are stored in memory. Programs that are of value, or programs that will be frequently used, are SAVEd on cassette tape. From your library, programs will be LOADed into computer memory for your use. Programs are also referred to as software.

After the screen has been cleared (see Lesson 1), type in the following program.

```
10   PRINT "THIS IS THE USA"
20   PRINT
30   PRINT "THIS IS THE"
40   PRINT "UNITED STATES"
50   PRINT "OF AMERICA"        (50 is a line number)
60   PRINT                     (PRINT is a program statement)
70   PRINT "THIS IS THE",
80   PRINT "USA"
999  END
```

(Lines 10 to 999 form a complete program.)

SAVING A PROGRAM

Type in RUN and press the RETURN key. The output from the program appears on the screen. Study the output in relation to the program statements. Now, type LIST and press RETURN. Notice that the program is LISTed on the screen. Now, type SAVE, and do the following steps. This will SAVE the program that is stored in memory onto a cassette tape.

1. Type in SAVE—*Do Not Press Return.*
2. Place a cassette into the tape recorder and rewind until the tape stops.
3. Press the stop/pause button.
4. Set the mechanical counter on the recorder to zero.
5. Forward the tape to a specific number on the counter (for example, number 5).
6. Set recorder volume to value 6 and the tone control to medium.
7. Press the record/play buttons (or the combination that will cause your recorder to record).
8. Now, press the RETURN (see Step 1, above) key on the computer. The cursor leaves the screen and the computer beeps. This indicates that the program is being SAVEd to tape.
9. When the recording is completed, the computer beeps again, and the cursor returns to the screen.
10. Press the stop/pause button on the recorder.

The program has been SAVEd to tape. To facilitate future location of this program, label the program on the tape cassette cover in the following manner:

1. Record the name and description of the program.
2. Record the starting number (on the tape counter) of the program.

3. Record the ending number (on the tape counter) of the program.
4. Record the volume and tone of the recording. (Generally, a volume of 6 and a medium tone, if using a Panasonic recorder, will satisfactorily SAVE and LOAD programs on the Apple II.)

Keeping a record of programs on tape aids in finding and LOADing programs. Loading only four programs onto each 15-minute tape is sufficient for program protection. Also, record programs on only one side of the tape. Valuable programs should be duplicated on separate tapes and stored in a safe place.

CHECKING THE PROGRAM

To check the program just recorded, reload the program into computer memory. The following routine is valid to either LOAD a program into memory or to reLOAD a program.

1. Type in NEW. This clears memory.
2. Type in LIST. This checks to see that memory is clear.
3. Type in LOAD, but *Do Not Hit Return.*
4. Rewind tape until it stops.
5. Set mechanical tape counter to read zero.
6. Run tape forward to counter number 4. (Program recording starts at number 5.)
7. Stop tape recorder.
8. Pull out Monitor Plug from recorder so sound can be heard.
9. Press Play button on the recorder.
10. When a shrill sound is heard, press plug into monitor.
11. Now, press RETURN (see Step 3).
12. The cursor leaves the screen, the computer beeps, and the program is LOADing.
13. When the program has completed loading, a beep is heard again, and the cursor returns to the screen.
14. Type either RUN to run or LIST to list the program.

After each operation, the RETURN key must be pressed to complete the operation. From this point on, when an operation is completed, you must press the RETURN key. Enough has been said about the RETURN key, so it will not be mentioned from now on.

VOLUME AND TONE

In most cases, a volume of 6 and a medium tone setting on the cassette recorder will produce a satisfactory LOAD or SAVE. A volume and/or tone setting that is too low will produce an ERR below the

LOAD or SAVE command shown on the screen. A volume and/or tone setting that is too high will produce a MEM FULL ERR message below the LOAD or SAVE entry. Persistent difficulty in LOAD or SAVE routines indicates the tape recorder should be checked to determine if the frequency of the recorder synchronizes with the frequency of the computer.

TAPES

Tapes should be of the highest quality and have a low background noise. Tapes that are of 15-minutes duration should be sufficient to record 4 programs of average length. Low-quality tape will give the user great difficulty in LOADing and SAVEing programs.

EXERCISE

Define any ten words from your computer dictionary. You do have a computer dictionary, don't you?

Programming and Print Rules

You should be able, after completion of this lesson, to:

1. Write a program in BASIC using PRINT statements.
2. Define and properly use six rules pertaining to PRINT statements.

VOCABULARY

BASIC—acronym for *Beginner's All-purpose Symbolic Instruction Code.*

BASIC command—commands that are executed immediately; they do not require line numbers. Examples are: RUN, LIST.

Format—the layout of a printed page.

Input—the process of transferring data, or program instructions, into memory from some peripheral unit.

Output—results produced by the computer.

PRINT—the statement that outputs data.

REM—abbreviation for Remark; it allows commentary in the program.

PROGRAM EXAMPLE

In this lesson, six rules pertaining to PRINT statements will be explained and discussed. These rules are important in formatting the output. The following program will be written and run in sections to give specific examples of the six rules. The complete program should be SAVEd on tape for future reference.

Rule 1

Anything in quotation marks is printed exactly as shown in the PRINT statement when the program is RUN.

```
5    REM-PROGRAM EXPLAINING 6 PRINT RULES
10   PRINT "THIS IS THE USA"
20   PRINT
999  END
RUN
THIS IS THE USA
```

Rule 2

Print statements with no punctuation following the closing quote cause the output to be printed on one line and cause the microcomputer to line feed (space down). Consecutive PRINT statements with no closing punctuation cause the output to be printed vertically, one output below the other.

```
30   PRINT "THIS IS THE"
40   PRINT "UNITED STATES"
50   PRINT "OF AMERICA"
999  END
RUN
THIS IS THE
UNITED STATES
OF AMERICA
```

Rule 3

A comma placed at the end of a PRINT statement places output in separate fields. Integer BASIC is designed to divide each line into 5 fields of 8 spaces each.

```
60   PRINT
70   PRINT "THIS IS THE",
80   PRINT "USA"
999  END
RUN
THIS IS THE      USA
```

Rule 4

A semicolon placed at the end of a PRINT statement causes the output to be packed (no spaces).

```
90   PRINT
100  PRINT "THIS IS THE";
110  PRINT "USA"
120  PRINT
999  END
RUN
THIS IS THEUSA
```

Rule 5

A comma between two items in a PRINT statement places the output in the first field and the next output in the next available field.

```
130   PRINT "THIS IS THE","USA"
140   PRINT
999   END
RUN
THIS IS THE          USA
```

Rule 6

A semicolon between two items in a PRINT statement causes the output to be packed (no space).

```
150   PRINT "THIS IS THE";"USA"
999   END
RUN
THIS IS THEUSA
```

Note that rules 3 and 5, and rules 4 and 6, give the same output, but are produced by a different program statement format.

EXERCISES

1. Define any ten words taken from your computer dictionary.

2. Write each of the six rules pertaining to PRINT statements ten times. (Repetition helps to impress the rules in your memory.)

3. Modify line 10 so that there are 10 spaces between "THE" and "USA."

4. Write and RUN a program using the six PRINT statement rules.

LESSON 4

Operators

After completing Lesson 4, you should be able to:

1. Write the order of precedence of arithmetic operators and how to modify that precedence.
2. Use constants and variables to do addition, subtraction, multiplication, division, and exponentiation.
3. Demonstrate PRINT output using variable names.

VOCABULARY

Arithmetic operator—symbols that instruct the microcomputer to do arithmetic operations in order to add, subtract, multiply, divide, and exponentiate.

Constants—in a program, constants are items of data which remain unchanged for each run.

Delimiters—signals that tell the computer how closely the results are to be printed, i.e., the comma and the semicolon.

Exponentiation—the power to which a quantity is raised.

DEL—abbreviation for Delete; it deletes the program line number and the program statement.

Integer—a whole number, i.e., one that does not contain a fractional component (whole, nonfloating point, etc.).

LET—statement that is called a replacement statement or an assignment statement. The number on the right of the equals sign is placed in the memory location whose name is specified on the left of the "equation."

Label—a variable designator of a memory location.

Memory location—the term describing the storage locations of a microcomputer.

Nested—one statement, routine, value, etc., contained inside another.

Precedence—the order in which things are done.

Reals—numbers with decimal points; also called decimals or floating-point numbers.

Variables—a character whose value is not fixed.

MATHEMATICAL OPERATIONS

The Apple II computer is designed to perform mathematical operations in a specific precedence as follows:

1. All negative numbers are operated on first. For example, in the expression $-3 + 2 = -1$, the -3 is a negative number. In the expression $3 - 2 = 1$, the -2 is not a negative number.
2. Exponentiations are operated on from left to right.
3. Division and multiplication are worked from left to right.
4. Addition and subtraction are worked from left to right.

To modify precedence, parentheses are used. If nested parentheses are used, the operation in the innermost parenthesis is performed first. Your problem is to divide 15 by $3 + 2$. If you write $15/3 + 2$, then $15/3 = 5 + 2 = 7$. To accomplish what you wanted, use parentheses to modify precedence, or $15/(3 + 2) = 3$. The rule that the computer follows is to do what is in the parenthesis first. If there are nested parentheses, the innermost parenthesis is executed first. The difference between two operations, one with and one without parentheses, is shown in the following examples.

```
15*(2+(3+2)*3)          15*2+3+2*3
= 15*(2+5*3)            = 30+3+6
= 15*(2+15)             = 39
= 15*17
= 255
```

EXAMPLE PROGRAM

Type NEW, LIST, and then type in the following program. This program is written in sections to demonstrate the replacement statement, arithmetic operators, arithmetic operations, and punctuation using variables. The entire program should be recorded on tape for future reference.

```
5    REM—PROGRAM USING ARITHMETIC OPERATORS,
6    REM—ARITHMETIC OPERATIONS, & PUNCTUATION
7    REM—USING VARIABLES FOR OUTPUT OF VALUES
```

```
10   LET A = 1+2+3+4+5
20   PRINT A
999  END
RUN
15
```

Line 10 is a replacement statement. The values on the right side of the equals sign are summed and placed in the memory location whose label is A and whose contents are 15 (Fig. 4-1). In this case, equals does not mean two equal values on opposite sides of the equals sign, but that the value on the right side of the equals sign is transferred to the left side of the equals sign. This is an operation (transfer) for the microcomputer to perform, and not an evaluation (decision). The equals is called the replacement operator and the LET statement is called the replacement statement. LET may be used to assign a constant value to a variable (example: LET A = 15), or it may be used to assign algebraic expressions to a variable (example: LET A = B*C+(D−E)/F). All values on the right side of the replacement statement are evaluated prior to being transferred to the left side.

Fig. 4-1. Memory location.

The line 20 PRINT A statement outputs 15, the value stored in memory under the variable label A.

Line 30, LET B = 9−5, is a replacement statement using the arithmetic operator (−) to perform subtraction.

```
30   LET B = 9−5
40   PRINT B
50   LET L = 6 : LET M = 7
```

Line 50 displays the use of the colon in Integer BASIC. The colon is used to separate two or more program statements that have the same line number. The colon increases program efficiency and reduces CPU (central processing unit) time needed to RUN the program. If line 50 is deleted (DEL 50) or changed, all necessary program statements must be replaced to maintain the program.

```
60   C = L*M
70   PRINT C
80   N = 25 : O = 5
90   D = N/O
100  PRINT D
```

Line 60 is a replacement statement without the LET statement. In Integer BASIC, LET is optional. Then, in line 80, the Apple keyboard prints an O with no slash through it. This is an alpha "oh" because a zero has a slash through it, i.e., Ø.

```
110   E = 6∧4
120   PRINT E
130   PRINT
```

The line 110 E = 6∧4 statement represents exponentiation.

```
140   PRINT A;B;C;D;E
150   PRINT
```

Line 140, with semicolons separating the variables, causes outputs where the variables are packed horizontally across the screen (PRINT Rule 4, Lesson 3). A RUN would be printed.

```
RUN
1544251296
```

A line with commas separating the variables,

```
160   PRINT A,B,C,D,E
```

causes the outputs to be printed horizontally across the screen, in 5 fields separated by 8 spaces between each (PRINT Rule 3, Lesson 3). A RUN of line 160 demonstrates the output.

```
RUN
15      4       42      5       1296
```

Line 170 A = B is a replacement statement and places the value in memory location B (a 4) into memory location A. The RUN of line 180 PRINT A,B,C,D,E causes the value of B (a 4) to be output into memory location A. The value of A is now 4 and the previous value of A (the 15) has been replaced.

```
170   A = B
180   PRINT A,B,C,D,E
190   A = C : A = D : A = E
200   PRINT A,B,C,D,E
999   END
RUN
15      4       42      5       1296    Line 160
4       4       42      5       1296    Line 180
1296    4       42      5       1296    Line 200
```

This lesson demonstrated that line 160 shows the values of A,B,C, D,E were outputted. Line 180 shows that the value of A (a 15) is now replaced by the value of B (a 4) as shown in the first and second fields of the printout. Line 190 demonstrates the value of A (a 4) being replaced by the value of E (1296) by shifting the value by steps; namely: A is replaced by C, A is replaced by D, and, then, A is replaced by E. The same results could have been achieved by simply A = E. A RUN of the program is shown as follows.

```
RUN
15
4
42
5
1296
1544251296
```

15	4	42	5	1296
4	4	42	5	1296
1296	4	42	5	1296

EXERCISES

1. Define ten words from your computer dictionary.

2. Write a program that demonstrates the rules of precedence, and then modify that program by using parentheses. Play computer and RUN the program before you RUN it on the computer.

3. Determine the values from Exercise number 2, above, and then shift the values A = B, B = A, etc., to practice the replacement statement.

Truncation and Integers

After completing this lesson, you should be able to:

1. Understand two deficiencies in Integer BASIC.
   A. Only integers will be accepted by the computer.
   B. Integer BASIC truncates.

VOCABULARY

Input—the process of transferring data, or program instructions, into memory from some peripheral unit.

Integers—a whole number, i.e., one that does not contain a fractional component.

Truncate—to suppress those digits of a number which are not significant, according to some predetermined requirement for accuracy in a result. Positive numbers drop the decimals and round down toward zero (8.87 truncates to 8). Negative numbers drop the decimals and round up toward zero (−8.75 truncates to −8).

Truncation error—an error arising from an inaccuracy in truncating a result.

PROGRAM EXAMPLE

Type in the following:

```
10   LET PI = 3.14
***  SYNTAX ERR
```

The program statement causes the computer to print *** SYNTAX ERR because Integer BASIC does not accept *reals* (a number with a decimal point or a floating point). Integer BASIC accepts only integers. This is one of the deficiencies of Integer BASIC. Type in several replacement statements containing reals to test the machine.

To overcome this deficiency, PI can be entered into the microcomputer as 314/100.

Now type in the following program.

```
10    PI = 314/100
20    R = 3
30    A = PI*R∧2
40    PRINT "AREA = (X)";A
50    PRINT
60    PRINT "AREA = (X)",PI*R∧2
70    END
RUN
AREA = 27
AREA =          27
```

Line 40 is an example of a concept not previously presented. Line 40 shows the example of a PRINT statement containing alpha characters and a logical operator in quotation marks and a variable separated by a semicolon. There is a space (X) between the closing quote so there will be a space between the = sign and the 27. The variable A outputs the constant 27; A = 27.

Line 60 demonstrates the PRINT statement containing alpha characters and a logical operator in quotation marks and a variable separated by a comma. As seen in the RUN, AREA = prints in the first field and the 27 prints in the next available field. Note, particularly, that either the variable A (line 40) or the algebraic expression PI*R∧2 (line 60) can print out the resultant numeral 27.

The result, AREA = 27, is an incorrect answer to the area of a circle problem. The correct answer is 28.26 (3.14*3*3 = 28.26). Thus, the answer 27 is incorrect and is caused by a truncation error.

$$\begin{aligned} PI &= 314/100, \text{ which truncates to } 3 \\ R \wedge 2 &= 9 \\ AREA &= \overline{27} \end{aligned}$$

There is a method that can be used to overcome both deficiencies in Integer BASIC and they will be explained in Lesson 6. The limits of Integer BASIC can be overcome with knowledge, practice, and programming finesse.

EXERCISES

1. Define ten words from your computer dictionary.

2. Using replacement statements, enter ten reals to check if the computer will accept them.

3. Originate and type in three programs using algebraic expressions in order to further study truncation.

Simulated Reals

After completing this lesson, Lesson 6, you should be able to:

1. Input numbers that simulate reals.
2. Output reals by simulating numbers that do not appear to be truncated.
3. Write interactive programs using the INPUT statement.
4. Write programs using GOTO and IF   THEN (decision) statements.
5. Use relational operators in decision statements.

VOCABULARY

Control---C—used to stop the computer. This will cause the prompt character and the blinking cursor to appear on the screen.

IF   THEN—a conditional statement; IF A = B THEN (GOTO) 999. If expression is true, then execute statement. If statement is false, do not execute. (GOTO statement is optional.)

Illegal—a statement or value that cannot be used by the microcomputer.

GOTO—a statement that causes a jump; thus, GOTO 50 causes an immediate jump to legal line number (for example, 50) specified by the expression.

INPUT—enters data into memory from input/output device. An I/O device.

32767 ERR—notice that an input statement or calculation has given a number greater than +32767 or less than −32767. To correct, input or generate smaller numbers.

Legal—a statement or value that is acceptable by the microcomputer.

Logical operator—a word or symbol representing some logical function that is to be applied to one or more associated operands (equal to, less than, greater than, etc.).

Operand—the item in an operation from which the result is obtained by means of defined actions.

Reals—a number with a decimal point.

Relational operator—a method used to compare quantities that are used to make decisions.

PROGRAM EXAMPLES

The next program is designed to calculate the area of a circle. It introduces the following new concepts.

1. Programming to simulate reals in Integer BASIC.
2. A method to truncate the output in Integer BASIC.
3. The use of INPUT, IF THEN (decision), and GOTO statements.
4. Relational operators.

Type in the following program on your microcomputer keyboard.

```
100   REM* CALCULATE THE AREA
110   REM* OF A CIRCLE
120   PI = 314
130   PRINT "INPUT RADIUS IN WHOLE #'S"
140   PRINT
150   INPUT R
160   IF R < = 0 THEN 999
170   REM* IF R < = 0 THEN PROGRAM ENDS
180   A = PI*R/\2 : REM* AREA OF A CIRCLE
190   PRINT
200   PRINT "AREA = ";A/100;".";
210   Z = A−(A/100*100) : IF Z < 10 THEN PRINT "0"; : PRINT Z
220   PRINT "TYPE A # FOR ANOTHER PROBLEM"
230   PRINT
240   PRINT "TYPE 0 TO END"
250   GOTO 150
999   END
RUN
INPUT RADIUS IN WHOLE #'S
?■   3■
AREA = 28.26
TYPE A # FOR ANOTHER PROBLEM
TYPE 0 TO END
?■   0■
```

Let us examine the program, section by section.

```
120   PI = 314
999   END
```

In line 120, the variable PI is entered as 314, a whole number. Then, the whole number (314) will be divided by 100, in line 200, so PI will be equal to 3.14, thus, bypassing a deficiency of Integer BASIC.

```
130   PRINT "INPUT RADIUS IN WHOLE #'S"
140   PRINT
150   INPUT R
```

Line 130 prepares the program user to input only whole numbers (integers) at the cursor that is next to the question mark (?) that was produced by the input statement. Line 150 is the input statement that produces a question mark (?) on the screen asking the user to input an integer. If a positive integer, greater than 0 (zero) or less than 11, is placed in the input field, the program runs until the answer is outputted. If a 3 is input, the answer AREA = 28.26 is printed out.

```
160   IF R < = 0 THEN 999
170   REM* IF R < = 0 THEN PROGRAM ENDS.
```

Line 160 is an IF THEN (decision) statement. If R (radius) is less than or equal to 0 (zero), then the microcomputer goes to 999 and the program ends. This decision statement is a method used for the microcomputer to check for legal or illegal input according to the program. A radius that is less than or equal to zero is an illegal value because a circle cannot have a negative area and, mathematically, you cannot multiply (or divide) by zero. If the radius entered is greater than 11, the Integer BASIC limitation produces a 32767 ERR comment. Line 160 places a limit on the computation by allowing neither negative numbers or a zero, and the language places a 32767 limit on the statement.

The relational operator is a method used to compare quantities that are used to make decisions.

=	Left expression "equals" right expression.
#	Left expression "does not equal" right expression.
>	Left expression "is greater than" right expression.
<	Left expression "is less than" right expression.
>=	Left expression "is greater than or equal to" right expression.
<=	Left expression "is less than or equal to" right expression.

Logical operators are related to relational operators and even though they have not yet been discussed, this is an ideal place to present them. A logical operator is a word or symbol to be applied to one or more operands. The numeric values used in logical evaluation are nonzero (1) and zero. The nonzero (1) represents yes or true. The zero represents no or false. The logical operators are:

NOT Logical negation of an expression.

AND In the statement IF A > B AND C > D THEN 999, both Expression 1 and Expression 2 must be true for the statement to be true.

OR In the statement IF A > B or C >D THEN 999, if either Expression 1 *or* Expression 2 is true, the statement is true.

Logical operators will be further used as you develop your programming techniques.

```
180   A = PI*R∧2
190   PRINT
200   PRINT "AREA = ";A/100;".";
210   Z = A−(A/100*100) : IF Z<10 THEN PRINT "0" : PRINT Z
```

Line 180 is the formula to compute the area of a circle. Line 200 is the command PRINT "AREA = ";A/100. The algebraic expression PI*R∧2, where PI = 314 and R = 3, computes to 2826. The A/100 expression divides 2826 by 100 and truncates the value to 28. (This is the first portion of line 200.) The "."; part of line 200 and the A−(A/100*100) part of line 210 places a period (.) after the 28 and computes

$$A-(A/100*100)$$
$$=2826-(2826/100*100)$$
$$=2826-28*100$$
$$=2826-2800$$
$$=26$$

The quantity 26 is the last part of the answer. It is added to the first part of the answer (28.) and the output is then printed out as "AREA = 28.26". (Notice in the computation that the first part of the value in the parenthesis is truncated to obtain the value 28 in the third line.)

The program command, RUN, outputs the following entries:

```
RUN
INPUT RADIUS IN WHOLE #'S
? ■   3 ■
AREA = 28.26
TYPE A # FOR ANOTHER PROBLEM
TYPE 0 TO END
```

If a 3 is typed for input, the answer is computed and produces the answer of 28.26.

A computer program runs sequentially according to the line numbers. The program runs (falls through) lines 210, 220, 230, 240, and 250, in order.

```
250  GOTO 150
```

A GOTO statement causes an immediate jump to the line number specified in the program statement. The statement GOTO 150 causes a jump to line 150 to INPUT R. Lines 220 and 240 cause instructions to be printed so the operator will know what to do when the INPUT question mark appears (from line 150).

```
150  INPUT R
160  IF R <= 0 THEN 999
```

Line 160 is a decision statement and the computer analyzes the zero input. Is the condition true? (Is R $\leq$ 0? Yes, 0 $\leq$ 0. Therefore, the condition is true.) Yes, the condition is true so the microcomputer branches to line 999 to end the program. If you had typed in the number 3, line 160 would have analyzed the number 3. (Is 3 $\leq$ 0? No, the number 3 is greater than zero, so the program falls through to line 180 to compute the area of a circle whose radius is 3.) Note that if the number is greater than zero, the program continues; if the number is zero or less than zero, the program ends.

Let's try another program to determine the volume of a sphere. This time, the IF THEN and GOTO statements will be referred to as loops. The program can be ended in one of two ways: (1) by typing a zero, or (2) by pressing Control---C and, then, RETURN to get out of the loop. In this example, an algebraic expression will be changed several ways to demonstrate how the accuracy of computation is changed by the way the formula is programmed.

Type in the following program.

```
10  PI = 314
20  INPUT "RADIUS = ",R
30  IF R< = 0 THEN 80
40  V = 4*PI/3*R∧3
50  PRINT "VOLUME = "; V/100;".";
60  Z = V-(V/100*100) : IF Z < 10 THEN PRINT "0"; : PRINT Z
70  GOTO 20
80  END
```

Line 20, which states INPUT "RADIUS = ",R, is a new form of input. Previously, the statement was INPUT R and it produced a question mark with no clarification. The input "RADIUS =",R outputs RADIUS = ? which gives a greater understanding of what the machine is asking. The RADIUS = term must be in quotation marks. The punctuation separating the closing quote and the variable in line 20 is a comma. A semicolon will give a SYNTAX ERR.

After the program has RUN with a positive integer between 1 and 4 (a 5 will produce a 32767 ERR) to get out of the loop without typing a zero, hold down both the CONTROL and C keys simultaneously, release, and then press RETURN. This action gains control of the microcomputer and ends the program. To continue the program, simply type RUN.

For the sake of brevity, line 40 will be typed four different ways with the RUN results entered to the right of the algebraic expression. Note that the correct answer to the computation of the volume of a sphere, whose radius is 3, is 113.04.

$$V = 4/3 \; PI*R\wedge3 \qquad \text{(The value of PI = 3.14)} \qquad = 113.04$$

The answers to the computation will vary greatly depending on the way the formula is programmed.

40	V = 133/100*PI*R∧3	(The value of PI = 314)	= 84.78
40	V = 4*PI/3*R∧3		= 112.86
40	V = (4*PI/3)*R∧3		= 112.86
40	V = (4*PI*R∧3)/3		= 32767 ERR

The best computer calculations are not as exact as the hand-calculator calculation. The results of a computer vary widely depending on how the formula is programmed. The inaccuracy of an answer is caused by the simulation of reals. A language (Applesoft) that accepts reals or floating points will give a more accurate result.

EXERCISES

1. Define ten new words from your computer dictionary.

2. Write a program to add the checks and subtract the deposits in your checkbook. Remember the 32767 limit.

LESSON 7

Catch-All

After completion of this lesson, you should be able to:
1. Define deferred and immediate execution.
2. Use AUTO to automatically give line numbers to program statements and, then, revert to typing line numbers manually.
3. Use LIST to list a program, a section of a program, or a single program statement.
4. Use the Edit function to change program statements.
5. Use DELete to erase sections of a program or program statements.

VOCABULARY

Deferred execution—is an execution that is not immediately executed. It begins with a line number. A sequence of deferred executions is called a program. Instructions in the deferred mode must appear in a line that begins with a line number. When the RETURN key is pressed, the line is stored in memory for future use. Instructions in the deferred mode are executed only when their line in the program is RUN. BASIC statements are deferred execution statements.

Immediate execution—is executed immediately when the RETURN key is pressed and released. Instructions in the immediate execution mode are typed without a line number. BASIC commands are synonymous with immediate execution.

AUTO—sets automatic line-numbering mode.

Edit—is used to arrange data into a format required for subsequent processing. Editing may involve the deletion of data not required.

MAN—stands for manual. It is the command that reverses the AUTO command which automatically places line numbers on program statements.

This is a catch-all lesson in which five concepts will be discussed. These concepts are peripheral to programming but are very important in making programming easier.

Deferred and immediate execution statements and commands are instructions that the microcomputer is designed to follow. Some commands, such as RUN, LIST, DEL, and PRINT, are executed immediately. Some statements, such as PRINT, LIST, or LET, are stored in memory for deferred execution. Some statements, such as PRINT, or LIST (10 LIST), take on a dual nature and are both immediate and deferred. It is sufficient for the beginning programmer to be able to define and understand the difference between immediate and deferred execution instructions.

The Apple II microcomputer has a convenient command that is used for automatic line numbering—AUTO. To use this function, type in NEW to clear the memory. Now, type AUTO 10. The AUTO 10 (both alpha and numeric quantities) must be typed in together. If you type in AUTO without typing the 10 (or the numeric quantity), a SYNTAX ERR appears on the screen and that frequent "beep" sounds to let the world know that you've made another error. Type in AUTO 10. The number 10 appears on the screen to the left of the blinking cursor. Then, type in the following program.

```
PRINT "THIS"
PRINT "IS"
PRINT "THE"
PRINT "USA"
END
RUN
*** SYNTAX ERR
```

We forgot to get out of the AUTO function. To stop the AUTOmatic numbering sequences, press Control---X, type in MAN, and press the RETURN key. Now type RUN.

```
RUN
THIS
IS
THE
USA
```

Control---X allows you to input line numbers not in the AUTO sequence. If you are just going to add line numbers out of sequence, do not type in MAN to come out of the AUTOmatic function.

Now, type in AUTO 1000,50 and, then, type in this program.

```
PRINT "THIS"
PRINT "IS"
PRINT "THE"
PRINT "USA"
END
```

Press Control---X, type in MAN, and

```
RUN
THIS
IS
THE
USA
```

The AUTO 1000,50 instruction starts the first line number at 1000 and increments each following line number by 50. Pretty nice function, eh?

Now that we have the AUTO function under control, let's look at the LIST function. LIST can be used in one of three ways. Refer to the previous program.

```
LIST
1000   PRINT "THIS"
1050   PRINT "IS"
1100   PRINT "THE"
1150   PRINT "USA"
1200   END
```

By typing LIST, the entire program is LISTed for the operator. Now, type LIST 1000,1100.

```
LIST 1000,1100
1000   PRINT "THIS"
1050   PRINT "IS"
1100   PRINT "THE"
```

LIST 1000,1100 lists only the line numbers 1000 to 1100. This is very important when you have a very long program and need to check different sections of the program.

Now type LIST 1000. Only line 1000 appears on the screen.

```
LIST 1000
1000   PRINT "THIS"
```

Suppose this program statement needs to be changed. You could type in DELete 1000, hit the RETURN key, and the statement would be deleted. However, if you wanted to change the statement, simply type,

```
1000   PRINT "THIS IS THE USA"
RUN
THIS IS THE USA      (Remember this program was in the computer and only line 1000
IS                   was changed.)
THE
USA
```

Another way to change line 1000 is to use the edit function.

```
LIST 1000
1000   PRINT "THIS IS THE USA"
```

For this operation, we will use the ESC key on the microcomputer keyboard. (ESC stands for ESCAPE, so we will use the word ESCAPE from now on.) To change line 1000, press the ESCAPE key and then the D key, in sequence. Notice that the cursor moves up one line on the screen. The ESCAPE key and the D key must be pressed, in sequence, each time to move the cursor up one line. This is a pure cursor move. The cursor is moved without affecting anything except the cursor. Press the ESCAPE and D keys again. Now the cursor rests over the 1 in 1000. Now press the ESCAPE key and the A key, in sequence. The cursor moves to the first 0 (zero) in 1000. Now, press ESCAPE and B. Press the ESCAPE key and the B key again. The cursor moves to the left of 1000. Now, press the ESCAPE key and then the C key. The cursor moves down one line on the screen. Did you put a letter C on the screen? You did? You must press the ESCAPE key before you press the letter key. To erase the letter C, place the blinking cursor over the C, and press the space bar. The space bar clears the letter C from the screen. The following action is occurring:

> ESCAPE---A moves cursor to the right
> ESCAPE---B moves cursor to the left
> ESCAPE---C moves cursor down
> ESCAPE---D moves cursor up

Now, back to the Edit function. Press ESCAPE, then D. The cursor should rest over the 1 in 1000. If it doesn't, place the cursor over the 1. Now, press the shift-right key. The cursor moves one space to the right (same as with ESCAPE---A). Again, press the shift-right key, and hold down the REPEAT key. The cursor moves rapidly to the right. Move the cursor to the A in USA. Whoops, you went too far, eh? Press the shift-left key. The cursor moves one space to the left. Again, press the shift-left key and hold down the REPEAT key. Move the cursor back to the T in THIS. The cursor should be to the right of the opening quote. Now type:

```
"THIS IS THE GOOD OLE USA"
RUN
THIS IS THE GOOD OLE USA
IS
THE
USA
```

Now type LIST 1000.

```
LIST 1000
1000  PRINT "THIS IS THE GOOD OLE USA"
```

Use the Edit function of pressing the ESCAPE-then-D key to place the cursor over the 1 in 1000. Now, press the shift-right key to move the cursor one space. It is very important to press the shift-right key once before you press the REPEAT key. If you press the REPEAT key before you press the shift-right key, you will repeat the last letter typed (in this case, D). Now, press the shift-right key and the REPEAT key to move the cursor to the space after A in USA (over the closing quote). Now type in the following.

```
, GOD BLESS HER AND KEEP HER WELL."
```

Press RETURN and type LIST 1000.

```
LIST 1000
1000  PRINT "THIS IS THE GOOD OLE USA,
      GOD BLESS HER AND KEEP HER WELL.
      "
```
(Note that the final quote falls on the third line of the statement.)

Notice that the microcomputer has shifted GOD BLESS HER AND KEEP HER WELL from the first column to the seventh column. The design of the machine causes the shift. This is a very important note to remember when editing on two or more lines of a print statement.

```
LIST 1000
1000  PRINT "THIS IS THE GOOD OLE USA,
      GOD BLESS HER AND KEEP HER WELL.
      "
```

Now change HER in the second line of the print statement to HIM. ESCAPE-then-D is pressed four times to place the cursor over the 1 in 1000. The shift-right key is pressed once. Then, the shift-right key and REPEAT are held down until the cursor is over the H in HER. HIM is typed in place of HER. The cursor is carried past the end of the third line and RETURN is pressed.

```
RUN
THIS IS THE GOOD OLE USA,        GOD BL
ESS HIM AND KEEP HER WELL.
```

Using the shift-right and REPEAT keys to repeat (move) from one line to another causes 7 spaces to be placed at the end of the first line, and the second line is started on line 1 with the 7 spaces between the end of the first line and the beginning of the second line. This is very distressing when editing a long program. One way to by-pass this deficiency is to use the ESCAPE-then-A function from the end of line 1 to the beginning of line 2.

Type in NEW and LIST and, then, retype line 1000.

```
1000  PRINT "THIS IS THE GOOD OLE USA, G
```

OD BLESS HER AND KEEP HER WELL."
1200   END

Now, LIST line 1000.

```
LIST 1000
1000   PRINT "THIS IS THE GOOD OLE USA,
         GOD BLESS HER AND KEEP HER WELL.
       "
```

Change HER in the second line to HIM by using the following method. Press the ESCAPE key and, then, the D key, in sequence, to move the cursor over the 1 in 1000. Press the shift-right key once. Press the shift-right and REPEAT keys until the cursor rests after the comma (,) after USA. Press the ESCAPE key and, then, the A key until the cursor rests over the G in GOD. Now, press the shift-right key and the REPEAT key until the cursor rests over the H in HER. Type in HIM. Press the shift-right key and the REPEAT key until the cursor rests after the period (.) after WELL. Press the ESCAPE and A keys until the cursor is past the closing quotation mark on the third line. Now LIST 1000.

```
LIST 1000
1000   PRINT "THIS IS THE GOOD OLE USA,
         GOD BLESS HIM AND KEEP HER WELL.
RUN
THIS IS THE GOOD OLE USA, GOD BLESS HIM
AND KEEP HER WELL.
```

By using the ESCAPE-then-A function from the end of one line to the first letter (or character) in the next line, the spacing of the output is retained. This feature should be kept in mind when editing programs.

Now type in the following:

```
1000   PRINT "THIS IS THE USA."
```

In editing functions, the cursor must be moved past the end of the line before the RETURN key is pressed. In line 1000, move the cursor over the I in IS.

```
1000   PRINT "THIS ■S THE USA."
```

In place of IS, type in ARE and press the RETURN key. A SYNTAX ERR appears and a beep sounds and line 1000 looks like this.

```
1000   PRINT "THIS ARE
*** SYNTAX ERR
```

The cursor must be moved past the end of the line before RETURN is pressed.

EXERCISES

1. Define ten new words from your computer dictionary.

2. Type in a program of your choice and practice using the functions discussed in this lesson. Practice the editing function until you feel you are proficient with it.

LESSON 8

Flowcharting

After you have completed this lesson, you should be able to:

1. Begin using logical thought in problem solving.
2. Flowchart simple problems by using flowchart symbols.

VOCABULARY

Bug—any mistake or malfunction of a computer program or system.

Logic—the science that deals with the formal principles of reasoning. In electronic data processing, the principles observed in the design of a computer system or of any particular unit. Principles pertaining to the relationships between elements in the unit concerned, without consideration of the hardware necessary to implement this design.

Logical—a term used in the context of operating systems to describe entities (files, resources) as they appear to the user, in contrast to physical files, etc., which are the actual entities as they exist. Logical entities are derived from physical entities by means of operating system software.

Hardware—the physical units of a computer system. The apparatus as opposed to the programs. Contrasted with software.

Logic flowchart—a chart representing a system of logical elements and their relationships within the overall design of a system or hardware unit. The representation of the various logical steps in any program or routine by means of a standard set of symbols. A flowchart produced before detailed coding for the solution of a particular problem.

Software—in its most general form, software is a term used, in contrast to hardware, to refer to all programs which can be used on a particular computer system.

THE PROBLEM

When you write a computer program, you solve a problem. The most basic approach to solving a problem is to first understand the problem. In the program to compute the area of a circle, the formula has been discussed and thought out in high school math. The knowledge simplifies the programming of the output. A program to compute three types of depreciation methods somewhat changes the problem for the nonaccountant. The first problem in programming is to understand the problem and its ramifications.

Once the problem is understood, the solution must be placed in the proper order and language so that the computer can obey your commands and produce an output according to your instructions. The computer can only output according to a specific input. You often hear the excuse, "It's the computer's error." Computers seldom (if ever) make errors; it is the human input that is in error. Computers are stupid but they are exacting. Many programmers pray for a DWIT (do what I think) program statement. The DWIT statement is not yet available in Integer BASIC, so we must do the best with what is available. Remember, the computer does exactly what you tell it to do, nothing more, nothing less.

THE PROGRAM

Once the problem, the language, and the computer are understood, all other problems are relatively simple. The program can now be written to solve the problem. However, there is a great semantic difference between noncomputerese and computerese. Equals was originally defined as one side being equal to the other side (3+2=5). In computerese, equals means that the left side of the equation is to be replaced by the right side of the equation (X=X+1), as in a replacement statement. Equals is also a logical operator in a decision statement (IF R = 0 THEN 99). The change in definition can be difficult for those whose minds are set from older days.

After the program has been written, the following question must be asked. "Does it solve the problem and give the desired results?" Hopefully, the answer is yes. If the answer to the area of a circle comes out to be a negative value, either the problem or the program must be reevaluated.

Once the results of the program are output, they must be checked for accuracy in relation to valid computational methods. If 2.5 *

$2 = 5$ and, through truncation and simulated reals, the computer produces an output of $2.5 * 2 = 4$, then these results are invalid for useful purposes. The "bugs" in the program must be rectified to produce valid, consistent, and usable results.

Has the program been documented with REM statements so that another person could RUN the program and understand the output? Have the variables been recorded so the computational formulas can be easily understood? Has the program been properly indexed so it can be easily located in the library? The answers to all these questions should be yes. Remember that it is easy to forget what problem a program solves, what the variables represent, and where the program can be located.

Finally, the program must be checked to see if an unusual input produces an undesirable output. If the decision statement is IF R = 0 THEN 99, and a negative number is input, what happens? In this case, the statement should be changed to IF R $<=$ 0 THEN 99. This avoids a negative area of a circle. As you learn more about programming, the more you will learn that the machine accepts only exact program statements. The microcomputer does only what you tell it to do and, therefore, you must always tell it exactly what to do.

FLOWCHARTS

Flowcharting, or logic flowcharting, is a technique for representing a succession of events in symbolic form. Flowcharting is the first step in logical program development. This aids in "thinking" the program through both from the problem and the microcomputer aspect. The steps represented in a flowchart encompass a variety of events that are related as to type. In data processing, flowcharts may be divided into two types—system flowcharts and program flowcharts.

System Flowcharts

System flowcharts, using symbols, show the logical relationship between successive events that use hardware. Such symbols (Fig. 8-1) include data input forms, such as magnetic tape, discs, and punched cards, and the output of data through printer terminals (hardcopy), magnetic tape, or disc.

Program Flowcharts

Program flowcharts show the logical relationship between successive steps in the program via diagrams. For most complicated programs, an outline flowchart will precede a detail flowchart. The outline flowchart is charted before the program is written.

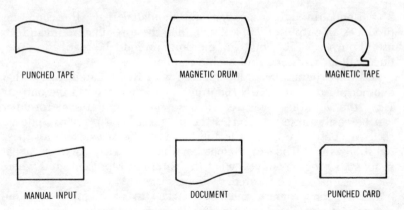

PUNCHED TAPE   MAGNETIC DRUM   MAGNETIC TAPE

MANUAL INPUT   DOCUMENT   PUNCHED CARD

Fig. 8-1. System flowchart symbols.

The purposes of an outline or initial flowchart are: (1) to show all input and output functions, (2) to show how inputs and outputs are to be processed, and (3) to show how the program will be divided into routines and subroutines.

The purposes of a detail or final flowchart are: (1) to interpret the detailed program specifications, (2) to determine the programming techniques to be used, (3) to provide direction for code and comments, and (4) to fix the program style for ease of interpretation.

Program flowcharting symbols usually conform to some standard set in which each symbol has a specific meaning. The flowchart symbols and their definitions are given in the following list.

PROGRAM FLOWCHART SYMBOLS

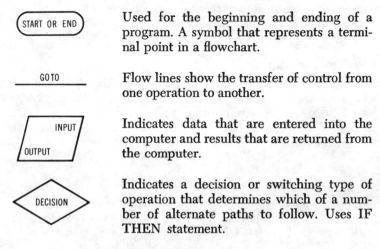

START OR END   Used for the beginning and ending of a program. A symbol that represents a terminal point in a flowchart.

GOTO   Flow lines show the transfer of control from one operation to another.

INPUT OUTPUT   Indicates data that are entered into the computer and results that are returned from the computer.

DECISION   Indicates a decision or switching type of operation that determines which of a number of alternate paths to follow. Uses IF THEN statement.

OPERATION	Operation or process symbol that represents any kind of processing function, such as initializing, counting, summing, or computing. Uses FOR NEXT, and LET commands.
PREDEFINED PROCESS	Indicates a sequence of program statement items in a list.
(1) CONNECTOR (1)	A symbol (pair) to represent the exit or entry from another part of the flowchart. It is used to indicate a transfer of control, from one point to another, that cannot be conveniently shown on a flowchart because of a confusion of connector lines, or because the flowchart is continued on another page.

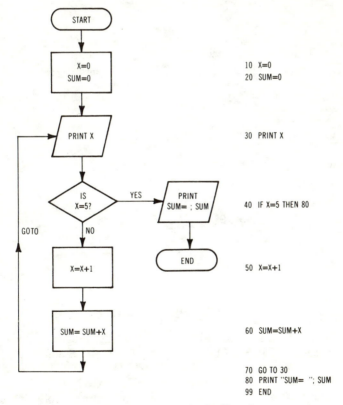

```
10  X=0
20  SUM=0

30  PRINT X

40  IF X=5 THEN 80

50  X=X+1

60  SUM=SUM+X

70  GO TO 30
80  PRINT "SUM= "; SUM
99  END
```

Fig. 8-2. Flowchart for Problem 1.

49

FLOWCHART EXERCISES

Problem 1

The flowchart and program for determining the sum of the integers from 1 through 5 is shown in Fig. 8-2. It uses a GOTO loop.

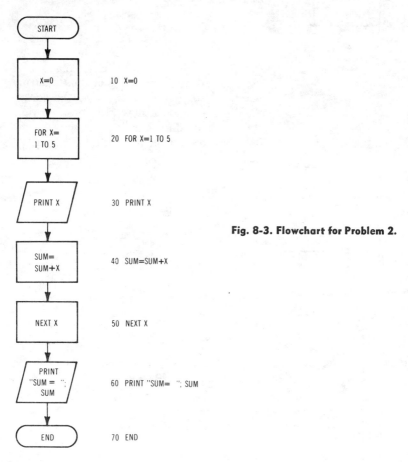

Flowchart	Program
START	
X=0	10 X=0
FOR X= 1 TO 5	20 FOR X=1 TO 5
PRINT X	30 PRINT X
SUM= SUM+X	40 SUM=SUM+X
NEXT X	50 NEXT X
PRINT "SUM = "; SUM	60 PRINT "SUM= "; SUM
END	70 END

Fig. 8-3. Flowchart for Problem 2.

Problem 2

A flowchart and program for the sum of the integers 1 through 5, which uses a FOR NEXT loop, is shown in Fig. 8-3.

Problem 3

For the final exercise, a flowchart and program to both determine the eligibility of, and to count the number of, applicants for operators

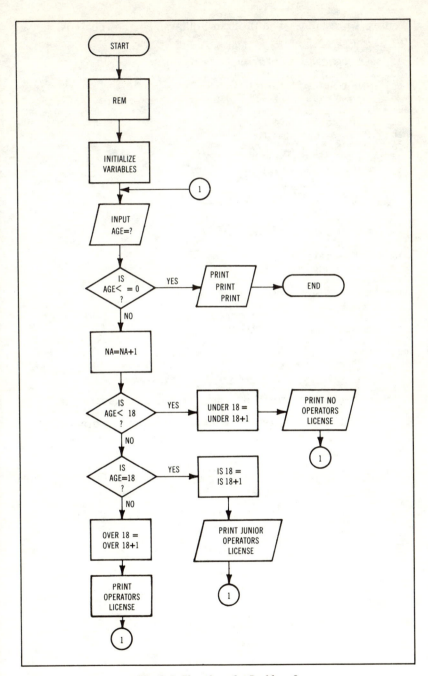

Fig. 8-4. Flowchart for Problem 3.

licenses is presented. The program follows. The flowchart is shown in Fig. 8-4.

```
10   REM* PROGRAM TO DETERMINE
20   REM* LICENSE ELIGIBILITY AND
30   REM* COUNT APPLICANTS
40   NA = 0 : UNDER 18 = 0 :
     IS 18 = 0 : OVER 18 = 0
50   INPUT "AGE = ",AGE
60   IF AGE < = 0 THEN 190
70   NA = NA + 1
80   IF AGE <18 THEN 130
90   IF AGE = 18 THEN 160
100  OVER 18 = OVER 18 + 1
110  PRINT "OPERATORS LICENSE"
120  GOTO 50
130  UNDER 18 = UNDER 18 + 1
140  PRINT "NO OPERATORS LICENSE"
150  GOTO 50
160  IS 18 = IS 18 + 1
170  PRINT "JUNIOR OPERATORS LICENSE"
180  GOTO 50
190  PRINT "TOT APP   UND 18    18
     OVER 18"
200  PRINT
210  PRINT NA, UN 18, IS 18, OV 18
220  END
```

EXERCISES

1. Define ten new words from your computer dictionary.

2. Flowchart, using the proper symbols, your path from your home to your favorite sports activity. Make a second one to your favorite restaurant. Do both an outline and a detailed flowchart.

3. Flowchart both the program to compute the area of a circle and the program to compute the volume of a sphere.

Loops and Counting Variables

After completion of this lesson, you should be able to:

1. Write simple programs using the GOTO loop.
2. Initialize variables and use counting variables within the program.
3. Determine how large programs are made up of small programs (program sections).

VOCABULARY

Conditional transfer—the IF   THEN statement is an example of a conditional transfer. If the condition is true, the transfer is executed. If the condition is false, the next statement is executed.

Counting variable—a replacement statement that is incremented to keep track of specific input values. An example is $NA = NA + 1$.

Documentation—specific comments used to clarify and/or record the program.

Flowcharting—is a technique for representing a succession of events in symbolic form.

Increment—a quantity which is added to another quantity.

Initialization—a process performed at the beginning of a program or subroutine to ensure that all indicators and constants are set to prescribed conditions and values before the routine is obeyed.

Unconditional transfer—a statement that causes an immediate jump to the designated line number. An example is GOTO.

PROGRAM EXAMPLE

The following program is designed to determine the eligibility of applicants for drivers licenses, according to their age. At first reading, the program may look strange with all the REMarks scattered throughout the program. (It is the same program that was flowcharted in Fig. 8-4 in the last chapter.) The program is designed so that it can be easily changed to introduce the concepts of initializing variables, summing variables, printing out totals of the summed variables, and program sections. Large programs are only little programs (program sections) fitted together. The first section of the program is the simple input of the applicant's age to determine eligibility for an operator's license. The first program revision will initialize the variable to count the total number of applicants (NA = 0), place a summing variable (NA = NA + 1) in the program, and print out the total number of applicants. The second revision will include initializing the remaining variables (UNDER 18 = 0, IS 18 = 0, and OVER 18 = 0), summing the three classes of applicants, and printing out the totals (Total Applicants, UNDER 18, 18, and OVER 18). The third part of the lesson is not a program revision but an explanation of program sections. Type in the following program:

```
10    REM*PROGRAM TO DETERMINE
20    REM*LICENSE ELIGIBILITY AND
30    REM*COUNT THE NUMBER OF APPLICANTS
40    REM*INITIALIZE VARIABLES
50    INPUT "AGE = ",AGE
60    IF AGE <= 0 THEN 190
70    REM*COUNTING VARIABLE
80    IF AGE <18 THEN 130
90    IF AGE = 18 THEN 160
100   REM*COUNTING VARIABLE
110   PRINT "OPERATORS LICENSE"
120   GOTO 50
130   REM*COUNTING VARIABLE
140   PRINT "NO OPERATORS LICENSE"
150   GOTO 50
160   REM*COUNTING VARIABLE
170   PRINT "JUNIOR OPERATORS LICENSE"
180   GOTO 50
190   REM*TOTALS HEADING
200   PRINT
210   REM*PRINT TOTALS
220   END
RUN
AGE = 16
NO OPERATORS LICENSE
AGE = 18
JUNIOR OPERATORS LICENSE
AGE = 20
```

OPERATORS LICENSE
AGE = 0

The output gives the license eligibility according to age. That is fine, because that is exactly what the program was designed to do. Now, in the first revision, the program will count the number of applicants and print out the total number of applicants. Change the following program statements by typing in the same line number and the new program statement.

```
LIST
40    NA = 0                        Initialize variable = 0
70    NA = NA + 1                   Counting variable
190   PRINT "TOTAL APPLICANTS"
200   PRINT
210   PRINT NA
```

Line 40 initializes the variable NA = 0. Line 170, NA = NA + 1, is a replacement statement that counts the total number of applicants. When processing the first applicant after NA has been initialized to zero, a 1 is added to NA to equal 1 $(0 + 1 = 1)$ and the 1 is placed into NA on the left side of the replacement statement. With the second applicant, the process is repeated $(1 + 1 = 2)$ and the results are placed in NA on the left side of the replacement statement. As each applicant's age is input, the counting variable is incremented by 1. This incrementing continues until a zero input causes a branch to line 190 (line 60 IF AGE $<= 0$ THEN 190) and causes a printout of the total number of applicants. At this point, the program ends.

The program again does what it is supposed to do. It separates the eligible applicants by age and it prints out the total number of applicants.

The second revision separates the eligible applicants by age, counts and prints out the total number of applicants, and lists those applicants that are UNDER 18, 18, and OVER 18.

```
LIST
40    NA = 0 : UNDER 18 = 0 : IS 18 = 0 : OVER 18 = 0
100   OVER 18 = OVER 18 + 1
130   UNDER 18 = UNDER 18 + 1
160   IS 18 = IS 18 + 1
190   PRINT "TOT APP   UND 18   18   OVR 18"
200   PRINT
210   PRINT NA, UNDER 18, IS 18, OVER 18
220   END
RUN
AGE = 16
NO OPERATORS LICENSE
AGE = 18
JUNIOR OPERATORS LICENSE
AGE = 20
```

```
OPERATORS LICENSE
AGE = 0
TOT APP    UND 18    18        OVR 18
3           1          1          1
```

The second revision adds three more counting variables to the program. Line 40 initializes the variables to zero; UNDER 18 = 0 : IS 18 = 0 : OVER 18 = 0.

```
100   OVER 18 = OVER 18 + 1
130   UNDER 18 = UNDER 18 + 1
160   IS 18 = IS 18 + 1
```

Lines 100, 130, and 160 add counting variables to keep track of those applicants who are in the three "age" brackets. Note that the counting variables are placed in the program sections that deal with a specific age group. The counting variables are incremented by 1 for each applicant in the UNDER 18, 18, and OVER 18 age group. When 0 is input, the program branches to line 190 to print both the total applicants and the number of applicants in the UNDER 18, 18, and OVER 18 range. The two program revisions are completed and can solve the problem according to a predetermined output.

As can be seen from the original program and the two revisions, big programs are little programs put together in related sections. The program section pertaining to UNDER 18 applicants is:

```
80    IF AGE <18 THEN 130
130   UNDER 18 = UNDER 18 + 1
140   PRINT "NO OPERATORS LICENSE"
150   GOTO 50
```

The program section dealing with those applicants who are 18 consists of the following lines:

```
90    IF AGE = 18 THEN 160
160   IS 18 = IS 18 + 1
170   PRINT "JUNIOR OPERATORS LICENSE"
180   GOTO 50
```

Then, the program section that deals with those applicants OVER 18 is written in the following lines:

```
90    IF AGE = 18 THEN 160        (NO causes a default to line 100)
100   OVER 18 = OVER 18 + 1
110   PRINT "OPERATORS LICENSE"
120   GOTO 50
```

Finally, the program section that deals with the AGE = 0, and which causes the program to print out the totals and, then, to end, consists of the following lines:

```
60    IF AGE = 0 THEN 190
190   PRINT "TOT APP   UND 18   18   OVR 18"
```

56

```
200  PRINT
210  PRINT NA, UNDER 18, IS 18, OVER 18
220  END
```

In the operators eligibility program, there are three age classifications—UNDER 18, 18, and OVER 18. There are, however, only two decision statements used to select the three categories. This is shown in Fig. 9-1. (IF AGE = 0 THEN 190 does not select an age category.)

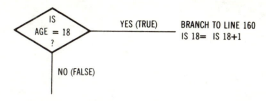

Fig. 9-1. Decision symbol showing the two possible decisions.

```
80   IF AGE <18 THEN 130
90   IF AGE = 18 THEN 160
100  OVER 18 = OVER 18 + 1
110  PRINT "OPERATORS LICENSE"
```

The three categories are selected as follows: (1) IF AGE < 18 selects those applicants under 18, (2) if AGE = 18 is true, the program branches to line 160, and (3) if AGE = 18 is false, the program defaults to line 100. (The rule of default will be discussed in the next lesson.)

That's how it's done. A program originally designed to do a simple function is expanded to do more complex functions.

EXERCISES

1. Define ten new words from your computer dictionary.

2. Write a program that will qualify airline pilots according to age. Under 21 (good to too young), 21 to 35 (good to prime), 35 to 60 (choice), and over 60 (administrator). Use a GOTO loop to make the program end smoothly. Write the program so it is revised twice. Original program is to separate the applicants by age. The first revision is to count the number of applications and print out the total number of applicants. The second revision is to count the total applicants, count the applicants by age classification, and print out the totals.

3. Develop a program using GOTO and IF THEN statements that are based on priority items concerning your job.

LESSON 10

Rule of Default and Decision Statements

After you have completed Lesson 10, you should be able to:

1. Explain the rule of default.
2. Write the three pairs of opposites in decision statements.
3. Use three rules for efficient programming using decision statements.

VOCABULARY

Default—the rule of default states that a computer program runs sequentially according to increasing line numbers unless a program statement causes a branch out of sequence.

DECISION STATEMENTS

There are three pairs of opposites that are used to reverse the logic of an **IF THEN** statement. They are:

1. $>$ is opposite $<=$
2. $<$ is opposite $>=$
3. $=$ is opposite #

Decision statements (IF THEN) operate on a true (YES or 1) or a false (NO or 0) basis. This is shown in Fig. 10-1. In a decision statement, a question is asked. If the answer to the question, "Is condition true?", is a NO (false or 0), the rule of default causes the pro-

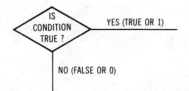

YES (TRUE OR 1)

NO (FALSE OR 0)

Fig. 10-1. Decision statement symbol.

gram to drop to the program statement following the question. If the answer to the question, "Is condition true?", if a YES (true or 1), the statement after THEN is performed. The following example is extracted from the operators license program in Lesson 8.

```
90    IF AGE = 18 THEN 160
100   OVER 18 = OVER 18 + 1
110   PRINT "OPERATORS LICENSE"
—
—
160   IS 18 = IS 18 + 1
170   PRINT "JUNIOR OPERATORS LICENSE"
```

In line 90, if the age input is 18, the decision is YES and the program branches to line 160. In line 90, if the age input is 29, the decision is NO and the program defaults to line 100.

For efficient programming, there are three rules for a decision statement. The rules, along with flowcharts and a written explanation, follow.

Rule 1

If the condition is true, do one thing. The flowchart is shown in Fig. 10-2.

```
20    X = 6 : Y = 4
30    IF X>Y THEN X = Y
```

Rule 2

If condition is true, DO two or more things. However, for efficient programming, this rule should be reversed. It should read,

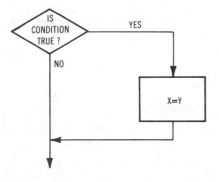

Fig. 10-2. Flowchart for Rule 1.

"if condition is NOT true, do two or more things to keep the program flowing efficiently." The first version is weak; this version is diagrammed in Fig. 10-3. Its program is listed as follows.

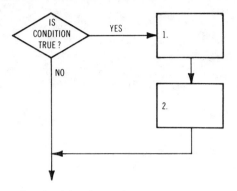

Fig. 10-3. Flowchart for the weak programming version of Rule 2.

```
30    IF X > THEN 50
40    GOTO 60
50    S = S + X + Y : C = C + 5
60    REM
```

The strong program is obtained by reversing the question so that the question is, "IS CONDITION FALSE?" This program is shown as follows and the flowchart for it is shown in Fig. 10-4.

```
30    IF X < = Y THEN 50
40    S = S + X + Y : C = C + 5
50    REM
```

Fig. 10-4. Flowchart for the strong programming version of Rule 2.

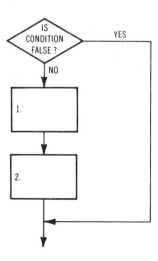

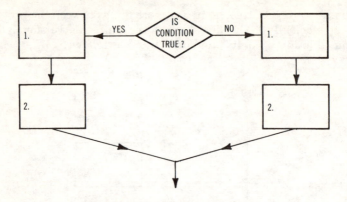

Fig. 10-5. Flowchart for Rule 3.

Rule 3

If the condition is true, DO one or more things, and if the condition is false, DO one or more things. The following list is the program for this rule. The program is diagrammed in the flowchart of Fig. 10-5.

```
30   IF X>Y THEN 50
40   S = S + 1 : C = C + 5 : GOTO 60
50   S = S + Y : C = C + 5
60   REM
```

EXERCISES

1. Define ten new words from your computer dictionary.

2. Flowchart the original and the two revisions of the operator's license program. Correlate the flowcharts with the program statements.

LESSON 11

General Outline of Programs

You should be able, after completion of this lesson, to:

1. Comprehend that all computer programs are written according to a general outline, but no outline will be specific for any program.

VOCABULARY

Data—a general expression used to describe any group of operands which denote any conditions, value, or state, i.e., all values and descriptive data operated on by a computer program but not the program itself. The word data is used as a collective noun. It is sometimes accompanied by a singular verb because "data are," while pedantically correct, is awkward to understand. (However, in this book, "data are" is the form used.) Data are sometimes contrasted with information, which is said to result from the processing of data, so that information derives from the assembly, analysis, or summarizing of data into a meaningful form.

Flag—is a variable used within a program to tell whether a previous condition has or has not occurred.

GOSUB—this causes a branch to a BASIC subroutine starting at the legal line number specified by the expression, such as GOSUB 800. Subroutines may be nested for up to 16 levels.

Menu—a method of using a terminal or display "list" of optional facilities, which can be chosen by the user in order to carry out different functions in a system.

Read—a statement used by the program to put data into memory. Not a function in Integer BASIC.

Subroutine—part of a program which performs a logical section of the overall function of the program and which is available whenever that particular set of instructions is required. The instructions forming the subroutine do not need to be repeated every time the program is run, but can be entered by means of a branch from the main program.

EXERCISE PROBLEM

The following outline for program structure must be considered very general and it should be understood that probably no program will ever comply with the outline. However, there must be a starting point to writing a program so this is the start. Some exceptions to the rule will be discussed after the outline has been written.

1. Computer program (general outline).
    A. Start the program.
    B. Initialize the variables; this is the assignment statement.
        (1) $C = 1$ Counting variable
        (2) $S = 0$ Summing variable
        (3) $F = 0$ Flag variable
    C. Print general headings.
    D. Menu.
    E. INPUT—READ.
    F. FOR GOTO loop beginning structure.
    G. Decision statements.
    H. Computation statements.
    I. Incrementing statements.
        (1) $C = C + 1$
        (2) $S = S + N$ N = number to be summed
        (3) $F = 0 : F = 1$
    J. PRINT—in this position, each time the loop is executed, the loop variable is printed.
    K. NEXT or GOTO loop end.
    L. PRINT—in this position, the accumulated loop totals are printed.
    M. Subroutines.
    N. DATA—certain languages have this statement.

Now that we have a general outline for program development, the FOR NEXT loop will be discussed, and then the loop structure will be changed to show how placement within the loop affects the output.

```
10   SUM = 0                  Initialize variable
20   FOR X = 1 TO 5           FOR  NEXT loop beginning
30   PRINT X                  PRINT loop variable
40   SUM = SUM + X            Summing statement
50   NEXT X                   End of loop statement
60   PRINT "SUM = ";SUM       PRINT outside loop—totals
70   END                      End of program
RUN
1
2
3
4
5
SUM = 15
```

The program generally conforms to the outline.

Lines 30 and 40 should be reversed according to the outline. Does it make a difference if they are reversed?

```
30   SUM = SUM + X
40   PRINT X
RUN
1
2
3
4
5
SUM = 15
```

No, the reversal of statements 30 and 40 within the loop make no difference. Generally, the PRINT X statement comes after the FOR statement.

Now, reverse lines 40 and 30 so as to return to the original program. From the original program, make these changes.

```
DEL 30
55   PRINT X
RUN
6
SUM = 15
```

The loop runs from 1 to 5 and it ended in line 50 (NEXT X). However, the computer did what it was told and printed the next integer in the series, namely number 6. The quantity, SUM = 15, is a proper value. Here, the general outline was violated and the program did not produce the desired result. Now, go back to the original program.

```
DEL 55
30   PRINT X
RUN
1
2
3
4
```

```
5
SUM = 15
```

Now, make the following changes.

```
DEL 60
45  PRINT "SUM = ";SUM
RUN
1
SUM = 1
2
SUM = 3
3
SUM = 6
4
SUM = 10
5
SUM = 15
```

The change produced about the same results but by placing the line 45 entry (PRINT "SUM = ";SUM) within the loop, it caused a sum output with each execution of the loop.

Go back to the original program.

```
DEL 45
60  PRINT "SUM = ";SUM
RUN
1
2
3
4
5
SUM = 15
```

Now, make the following changes to the original program.

```
DEL 10
25  SUM = 0
RUN
1
2
3
4
5
SUM = 5
```

In this case, the summing variable was initialized to zero each time the loop was processed, so the final value was SUM = 5. Thus, the initialized variable must be outside the loop or it will be reset to zero each time the loop is executed.

These examples demonstrate the validity of the general program outline, but stress the importance that each program is different and the program statements must be placed in the proper order for each program to produce the desired output. The initial problem in programming is to understand the problem. If you understand the problem, the next step is to determine what output is desired and in what format. These two solutions will help you greatly in writing the program.

EXERCISES

1. Define ten new words from your computer dictionary.

2. Type in the GOTO loop program given in Lesson 8 and change the sequence of the line numbers to analyze what effect these changes have on the output.

3. Type in the operator's license program given in Lesson 9. Rearrange the decision statements to determine how these changes affect blocks within the program. Lines 100, 110, and 120 are a block. Lines 130, 140, and 150 are a block. Lines 160, 170, and 180 are a block. Lines 190, 200, 210, and 220 are a block.

LESSON 12

Playing Computer

After the completion of this lesson, you should be able to:

1. Play computer and RUN a program manually to determine the output.
2. Play computer to discover why a program does not run or why it does not run properly.
3. Use the TRACE function to aid in debugging programs.
4. Use the NOTRACE function to counter the TRACE function.

VOCABULARY

Bug—any mistake or malfunction of a computer program or system.
Debugging—the technique of detecting, diagnosing, and correcting errors (also known as bugs) which may occur in programs or systems (both hardware and software).
NOTRACE—turns off the TRACE debug mode.
Pass—is a single execution of a program loop. It is also the passage of magnetic tape past the Read head.
TRACE—sets the debug mode that displays each line number as it is executed.

EXERCISE PROGRAM

The primary purpose of this lesson is to teach you to play computer. When you play computer, you take a program and run it both mentally and manually to determine the output or to debug it. It is very important that you learn to think like a computer if you are going to understand and outsmart this exacting machine. When you play computer, you RUN the program exactly as it is written. If the rule of default applies, use the rule of default. If the program uses a decision statement, you must make the proper decision to branch or default. You should make up a table to determine how the variables change with each pass. The following program should be RUN several times without the aid of a computer so that you will be able to get the feel of what a computer does. The variable table should be completed before the program is RUN by the computer.

```
10   REM*PROGRAM TO PLAY COMPUTER
20   A = 5 : B = 10 : C = −10
30   IF C > 0 THEN 130
40   IF B > A THEN 90
50   IF C < = 0 THEN C = C + 1
60   B = B − 2
70   PRINT A,B,C
80   GOTO 30
90   A = A + 1
100  C = C + 2
110  PRINT A,B,C
120  GOTO 30
130  C = C − 10
140  PRINT A,B,C
150  END
```

Good luck, and don't fudge on playing computer. This is a very important lesson.

Chart 12-1 is a variable chart that will allow you to compute the output and keep a record of your calculations.

Chart 12-1. Variable Chart

Assigned Value of Variables	A	B	C
From Line 20	5	10	−10
Values—1st pass			
Values—2nd pass			
Values—3rd pass			
Values—4th pass			
Values—5th pass			
Values—6th pass			
PRINT A,B,C			

TRACE FUNCTION

After you begin to feel comfortable running the program mechanically, add the following line to the program. Type in line 5 TRACE. A TRACE function prints the line number sequence on the screen as well as the output. In this way, the exact sequence of the program can be traced. This can be very educational in seeing how the program progresses. The TRACE function is very useful for debugging a program. If you have a program that is STOPPED AT 120, for example, the TRACE function can aid in determining why the program stopped. Did you have overlapping loops? Did you have a FOR with no NEXT? Did you have an IF   THEN 90, and there was no line at 90 for the branch? There are a zillion reasons as to why bugs stop a program from running. The TRACE function aids in debugging these problems.

NOTRACE FUNCTION

TRACE has a counterfunction called NOTRACE. The TRACE function must be removed from a program by typing in the same line number that TRACE has, and then typing in NOTRACE.

If the line number five reads   5   TRACE
    type in the line   5   NOTRACE (this removes TRACE).
To remove NOTRACE, delete line 5.

THE COMPUTER RUN

Are you sure you have correctly outputted the results manually? The following is the RUN and TRACE of the play computer program.

```
RUN
6        10      −8
7        10      −6
8        10      −4
9        10      −2
10       10      0
10       8       1
10       8       −9
```

(TRACE)								
#10	#20	#30	#40	#90	#100	#110	6	10
−8								
#120	#30	#40	#90	#100	#110		7	10
−6								
#120	#30	#40	#90	#100	#110		8	10
−4								
#120	#30	#40	#90	#100	#110		9	10
−2								
#120	#30	#40	#90	#100	#110		10	10
0								
#120	#30	#40	#50	#60	#70		10	8
1								
#80	#30	#130	#140		10		8	−9

EXERCISES

1. Define ten new words from your computer dictionary.

2. Play computer and run the "area of a circle," given in Lesson 6, manually. Also, run the "volume of a sphere" given in the same lesson. After you have completed this, type the programs into your microcomputer and TRACE the programs.

LESSON 13

Subscripted Variables

You should be able, after completion of this lesson, to:

1. Set DIMension limits using constants and variables.
2. Write programs using subscripted variables for numeric lists.
   A. To output a list as it is input.
   B. To output a list in reverse order.
   C. To operate on numbers in the list.
   D. To total the numbers in the list.

VOCABULARY

DIM—the DIM (dimension) statement causes the Apple II to reserve memory for the specified variables. For number arrays, Apple reserves approximately 2 times the amount of the expression in bytes of memory, limited only by available memory. For a string, arrays must be in the range of 1 to 255 characters.

List—any printing operation in which a series of records, on a file or in memory, are printed one after another.

Operate—a defined action by which a result is obtained from an operand.

Subscripted variable—a type of array. An arrangement of items of data, each of which is identified by a key or subscript. Constructed in such a way that a program can examine the array in order to extract data relevant to a particular key or subscript. The dimension of an array is the number of subscripts necessary to identify an item; e.g., if an array consists of the days of the week, the dimension statement subscript would be 7.

EXAMPLE PROBLEM

This lesson introduces a new type of variable—the subscripted variable for numeric lists or arrays. As you may remember, simple BASIC variables must begin with an alpha character from A to Z, and may be followed by an alpha character from A to Z, or by any numeric character from 1 to 9, and 0 (zero). The alpha and numeric characters must number less than 100. This information is similar to the question, "How fast can an elephant run?", but it might be important later during programming.

Fig. 13-1 and the following short notation shows several subscripted variables. Subscripted variables consist of a variable and a character in parenthesis. Compare these with the list of simple variables immediately following.

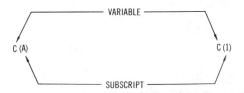

Fig. 13-1. Subscripted variables.

SUBSCRIPTED VARIABLES   C(A)   X(9)   CX(4)   G3(H)
SIMPLE VARIABLES   CA   X9   CX4   G3H

It should be noted that the variables A, (A(0)), AB, and A(B) can all be used in the same program successfully. A subscripted variable (like a simple variable) reserves a memory location using a label and the contents.

Five subscripted variables, with the memory location label of C(A), are listed in Table 13-1. Note that there are no values in the contents. For clarity, C(A) represents C(1), C(2), C(3), C(4), and C(5).

Table 13-1. Subscripted Variables

LABEL	CONTENTS
C(1)	
C(2)	
C(3)	
C(4)	
C(5)	

Suppose the contents of the memory locations, whose label is C(A), are filled with random numbers. LET C(1) = 8, LET C(2) = 5, LET C(3) = 19, LET C(4) = 1, and LET C(5) = −8. The five memory locations, whose labels are C(A), and their contents

Table 13-2. Subscripted Variables

LABEL	CONTENTS
C(1)	8
C(2)	5
C(3)	1
C(4)	19
C(5)	−8

now look like that shown in Table 13-2. The subscripted variable, or array, is now filled with a list of numbers.

When you remember that the subscript of the variable can be a variable, such as C(A), or a constant, like C(1), you begin to realize what a powerful tool the single subscripted variable turns out to be.

IF A = 1	THEN C(A) = C(1)
IF A = 2	THEN C(A) = C(2)
IF A = 3	THEN C(A) = C(3)

Subscripted variables give great processing power to the microcomputer, and as you will learn, they make the job much easier for the programmer.

To practice the conversion of using constants and variables in the subscripted portion of subscripted variables, complete the following exercise.

L(1)	2	N(1)	6	P	1
L(2)	5	N(2)	3	Q	2
M(3)	7	O(3)	1	R	3
M(4)	−2	O(4)	4	S	4

L(1) =	P =	L(P) =
L(2) =	Q =	O(R) =
M(R) =	N(Q) =	N(Q) =
M(S) =	M(S) =	N(P) =

2	1	2
5	2	1
7	3	3
−2	−2	6

A DIMension statement is necessary to create an array (subscripted variable). The DIM statement causes the Apple II to reserve memory locations for the specified subscripted variables or constants. DIM A(20) reserves 20 memory locations for the variable A. DIM A(N) reserves N memory locations for the variable A. N is used as a number that is to be inputted in a FOR NEXT loop. N is the amount of numbers that will be in a specific list. A typical DIMensioned statement is FOR X = 1 to N.

PROGRAM FOR SUBSCRIPTED VARIABLES

The following program and the RUN are typed for easy reference. The program deals with four ways to use subscripted variables. These are: (1) to print out a list of numbers as it is input into the computer, (2) to print the list backwards, (3) to operate on numbers within the list, and (4) to total the numbers in the list. Each section of the program will be discussed separately.

```
100   REM*SUBSCRIPTED VARIABLES
110   REM*FOUR WAYS TO USE THEM
120   REM*INPUT N NUMBERS
130   INPUT "HOW MANY NUMBERS ",N
140   DIM L(N)
150   FOR K = 1 TO N
160   PRINT "NUMBER";K;"=";
170   INPUT L(K)
180   NEXT K
190   PRINT "PRINT LIST AS INPUT" : PRINT
200   FOR A = 1 TO N
210   PRINT L(A),
220   NEXT A
230   PRINT : PRINT
240   PRINT "PRINT LIST BACKWARD" : PRINT
250   FOR B = N TO 1 STEP −1
260   PRINT L(B),
270   NEXT B
280   PRINT : PRINT
290   PRINT "TO OPERATE ON THE NUMBERS" : PRINT
300   PRINT "C    L(C)    L(C)+5    C∗L(C)    L(C)∧2"
310   FOR C = 1 TO N
320   PRINT C, L(C), L(C)+5, C∗L(C), L(C)∧2
330   NEXT C
340   PRINT
350   PRINT "THE LIST IS TOTALED"
360   T = 0
370   FOR D = 1 TO N
380   T = T + L(D)
390   NEXT D
400   PRINT "TOTAL OF THE LIST = ";T
999   END
RUN
```

```
HOW MANY NUMBERS ? 4
NUMBER 1 = 5
NUMBER 2 = 8
NUMBER 3 = 3
NUMBER 4 = 7
PRINT LIST AS INPUT
5    8    3    7
PRINT LIST BACKWARD
7    3    8    5
TO OPERATE ON THE NUMBERS
C    L(C)    L(C)+5    C*L(C)    L(C)/\2
1    5       10        5         25
2    8       13        16        64
3    3       8         9         9
4    7       12        28        49
THE LIST IS TOTALED
TOTAL OF THE LIST = 23
```

In programs dealing with subscripted variables, the variable must remain the same throughout the program. If the variable is L and the subscript is A, for a subscripted variable of $L(A)$, the L must remain the same throughout the program but the subscript may change. The subscript is the loop variable (FOR A = 1 TO N) in the subscripted variable $L(A)$. The subscript is either the loop variable or a character at a specific location in the list.

The first section of the program sets the DIMension statement $L(N)$. The L is the list variable, and the (N) is the subscripted variable that allows a flexibility to input lists of different quantities of numbers.

```
130    INPUT "HOW MANY NUMBERS",N
140    DIM L(N)
150    FOR K = 1 TO N
160    PRINT "NUMBER";K;"=";
170    INPUT L(K)
180    NEXT K
```
(How many numbers are there to be in the list? There is a maximum of 32767.)

This section of the program (lines 130 to 180) sets up the amount of numbers in the list and the numbers in the list. A RUN of lines 130 to 180 would look like this.

```
RUN
HOW MANY NUMBERS? 4
NUMBER 1 = 5
NUMBER 2 = 8
NUMBER 3 = 3
NUMBER 4 = 7
```

The list is now stored in memory and looks like this.

LABEL	CONTENTS
L(1)	5
L(2)	8

L(3)	3
L(4)	7

The second section of the program (line 190 to 230) outputs the list as it was input.

```
190   PRINT "PRINT LIST AS INPUT" : PRINT
200   FOR A = 1 TO N
210   PRINT L(A),
220   NEXT A
230   PRINT : PRINT
RUN
PRINT LIST AS INPUT
5     8     3     7
```

Line 200 uses the variable N to represent the amount of numbers in the list. This is shown by the statement FOR A = 1 TO N. In this case, there are four numbers in the list, so N = 4. Line 210, PRINT L(A), prints out the numbers in the list. Without subscripted variables, the programmer would have to write PRINT L(1), L(2), L(3), and L(4).

The third section of the program (lines 240 through 280) output the list of numbers in reverse order.

```
240   PRINT "PRINT LIST BACKWARD" : PRINT
250   FOR B = N TO 1 STEP −1
260   PRINT L(B),
270   NEXT B
280   PRINT : PRINT
RUN
PRINT LIST BACKWARD
7     3     8     5
```

Line 250, which says FOR B = N TO 1 STEP −1, is the loop format to output the numbers in reverse order by increments of one. Here, the PRINT L(B), in line 260, takes a list of numbers from their specific memory locations and prints them in reverse order.

The fourth section of the program (lines 290 to 340) does mathematical operations on the list of numbers. Any legal function used in Integer BASIC can be used on the list of numbers. In this case, the numbers in the list are printed, 5 is added to each number in the list, the number in the list is multiplied by the loop variable, and each number in the list is squared (multiplied by itself).

```
290   PRINT "TO OPERATE ON THE NUMBERS" : PRINT
300   PRINT "C    L(C)    L(C)+5    C*L(C)    L(C)∧2"
310   FOR C = 1 TO N
320   PRINT C, L(C), L(C)+5, C*L(C), L(C)∧2
330   NEXT C
340   PRINT
RUN
TO OPERATE ON THE NUMBERS
```

C	L(C)	L(C)+5	C*L(C)	L(C)$\wedge$2
1	5	10	5	25
2	8	13	16	64
3	3	8	9	9
4	7	12	28	49

The fifth section of the program totals and then prints the total of the numbers in the list.

```
350  PRINT "THE LIST IS TOTALED"
360  T = 0
370  FOR D = 1 TO N
380  T = T + L(D)
390  NEXT D
400  PRINT "TOTAL OF THE LIST = ";T
999  END
RUN
THE LIST IS TOTALED
TOTAL OF THE LIST = 23
```

EXERCISES

1. Define ten new words from your computer dictionary.

2. Write a program from scratch demonstrating the use of subscripted variables. (Look at the examples if you wish.) The subscripted variables in your program are to be used to (1) input a list of N numbers, (2) print out the list as input, (3) print the list backward, (4) operate on the numbers in the list, and (5) total the numbers in the list.

MIN-MAX and SORT

After completion of this lesson, you should be able to:

1. Find the minimum number and the maximum number from a list.
2. Use one-line-number multiple-program statements separated by colons for efficient programming.
3. Use the same variable for several different loops throughout the program.
4. Sort a list of items.

VOCABULARY

Sort—to arrange a list or lists of items in some order.

EXAMPLE PROBLEM

The problem to be solved by this program is to select and print the minimum (smallest) number and the maximum (largest) number from a list of numbers. The list of N numbers is input as the subscripted variable $L(J)$. On the initializing condition, the first number in the list is placed in the MAX memory location. If the first number in the list is an 8, the memory will be as pictured in Fig. 14-1.

The rest of the numbers in the list are then compared with the MIN and MAX memory locations. If the number in the list is greater than MAX, it replaces the number in MAX. If the number in the list is less than MIN, it replaces MIN. This comparison continues until all numbers in the list have been compared to MIN and MAX, and the minimum and maximum numbers in the list are in the proper MIN-MAX memory locations.

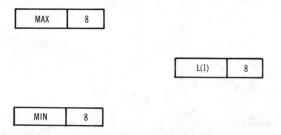

Fig. 14-1. Example of MIN–MAX locations in memory.

The program is written with multiple program statements per line number, with each separated by a colon. This is one method of increasing programming efficiency, as the computer takes less time to run the program since it is processing fewer numbers.

The loop variable and the subscript variable J is used throughout the program. This is done to demonstrate that the same variable can be used over and over again in the same program in order to decrease the amount of memory used.

One other point. The variable MIN is the value of the minimum or smallest number in the list. MAX is the value of the maximum or largest number in the list. MNS is the value of the subscript where the minimum number in the list is located. MXS is the value of the subscript where the maximum number in the list is located.

$$\text{LIST} \quad \begin{array}{l} L(1) = 8 \\ L(2) = 4 \\ L(3) = 7 \\ L(4) = 3 \end{array}$$

MAX = 8   Value of the maximum number.
MIN = 3   Value of the minimum number.
MXS = 1   Value of the subscript where the maximum number is stored; $L(MXS) = L(1)$.
MNS = 4   Value of the subscript where the minimum number is stored; $L(MNS) = L(4)$.

A MIN-MAX PROGRAM

Now, type in the program, RUN it, and INPUT a list of N numbers.

```
100   REM*PROGRAM TO SELECT MIN
110   REM*MAX NUMBERS FROM A LIST
120   INPUT "HOW MANY NUMBERS", N : DIM L(N)
130   FOR J = 1 TO N : PRINT "L(";J;")=" : INPUT L(J) : NEXT J : T = 1
140   PRINT "THIS IS THE ORIGINAL LIST" : PRINT
150   FOR J = 1 TO N : TAB T : PRINT "L(";J;")="; L(J); : T = T + 10 :
```

```
      IF T<31 THEN 160 : T = 1 : PRINT : PRINT
160   NEXT J : PRINT : IF T>1 THEN PRINT
170   MAX = L(1) : MIN = L(1)
180   MXS = 1 : MNS = 1
190   T = 2
200   FOR J = T TO N
210   IF L(J)<MIN THEN MIN = L(J) : IF L(J)>MAX THEN MAX = L(J)
220   IF L(J)<L(MNS) THEN MNS = J : IF L(J)>L(MXS) THEN MXS = J
230   NEXT J
240   PRINT "MAX IS"; MAX; "AND MIN IS"; MIN : PRINT
250   PRINT "L(";MXS;") IS THE MAX AND L(";MNS;") IS THE MIN" : PRINT
260   PRINT "YOU SEE MXS ="; MXS; "BECAUSE L(";MXS;") IS THE MAX"
270   PRINT "SIMILARLY, MNS ="; MNS; "BECAUSE L(";MNS;") IS THE MIN"
280   LIST 260, 270
999   END
RUN
HOW MANY NUMBERS? 4
L(1) =?8
L(2) =?5
L(3) =?19
L(4) =?−56
THIS IS THE ORIGINAL LIST
L(1) = 8   L(2) = 5   L(3) = 19
L(4) =  −56
MAX IS 19 AND MIN IS −56
L(3) IS THE MAX AND L(4) IS THE MIN
YOU SEE MXS = 3 BECAUSE L(3) IS THE MAX
SIMILARLY, MNS = 4 BECAUSE L(4) IS THE MIN
   260      PRINT "YOU SEE MXS ="; MXS; "BECAUSE L(";MXS;") IS THE MAX
   270      PRINT "SIMILARLY, MNS ="; MNS; "BECAUSE L(";MNS;") IS THE MIN
```

Although the program has only 20 line numbers, it has tremendous power for selection. Lines 100 and 110 are REMark lines that document the problem statement. Line 120 is the INPUT statement that asks the question, "How many numbers are to be in the list?" DIM L(N) is the dimension statement that reserves memory for N numbers in list L.

Line 130 begins with the loop to input N numbers in the list. Print "L(";J;")="; is an interesting variation of a PRINT statement in that "L(" prints out the variable and one side of the parenthesis while ;J; prints out the subscript value, and ")=" prints out the other side of the parenthesis and the = (equals sign) to input the number in the L(J). INPUT L(J) and the NEXT J completes the loop to input the list of numbers. T = 1 sets the value of T to be used in the TAB statement that is used to output the numbers in the list.

Line 140 causes the heading of "THIS IS THE ORIGINAL LIST" to be printed.

Line 150 starts with FOR J = 1 TO N to print out the original list. TAB T (T = 1) sets the first printing to column 1 for L(1). After L(1) is printed in column 1, T = T + 10 causes the printer to space 10 spaces to print L(2), etc., until the list is printed. The entry IF

T<31 THEN 160 causes the next number in the list to be printed on the next line, if the last list number was started after the thirty-first column on the screen. Then, T is again set (T = 1) so that the first list number on the next line is printed starting at column number 1.

The line 160 entry of NEXT J completes the loop, the PRINT closes out the line, and, then, IF T>1 skips a line.

Line 170 is used as an initializing condition to place the numerical value (number) that is in L(1) in both the MAX and the MIN memory locations. From this location, all numbers in the list will be compared to MAX and MIN. If the number compared to MAX is greater than maximum, the larger number will be placed in this memory location. If the number compared to MIN is less than minimum, then the smaller number will be placed in this location.

Line 180 is a different way to select MAX and MIN. It is included as a training exercise in order to store the value of the subscript that holds the MAX and MIN numbers.

The line 190 T = 2 entry sets the variable for the loop shown in line 200—FOR J = T TO N. The loop could have read FOR J = 2 TO N, so the T = 2 entry is included in the program to reenforce the learning experience of initializing variables. Variable T starts at 2 because there is no need to compare MAX and MIN to L(1).

Line 210 consists of two decision statements that compare the numbers in the list to the number stored in MIN, which starts with the value of L(1). The entry, IF L(J)<MIN THEN MIN = L(J), compares the numbers in the list to the number in L(1). The smaller number is placed in the MIN memory location. The entry, IF L(J)> MAX THEN MAX = L(J), also compares the numbers in the list to the number in L(1), and the larger number is placed in the MAX memory location.

Line 220 is unnecessary in this program to determine MIN and MAX from a list of numbers. It is placed in the program as a training exercise and the statements store the value of the subscript where MIN and MAX can be found.

Line 230 completes the loop. Then, lines 240, 250, 260, and 270 output the results and partially explain what the program accomplishes.

The line 280 entry of LIST 260, 270 demonstrates that LIST can be a deferred command. Also, lines 260 and 270 further explain the output and help give it clarity.

A MIN PROGRAM

The following two programs, (1) to select the minimum (smallest) number from a list of N numbers, and (2) to sort a list of numbers from the least to the greatest, are somewhat repetitious. Sorting, merging, and creating new lists are always a problem in programming and data processing. However, repetition of programs with a similar output will display the problem of sorting from three different perspectives. The MIN-MAX program is a training program used to select the MIN-MAX quantities by numerical value and by subscript value. The MIN program eliminates the training aspect and produces the MIN number in a list of N numbers. The SORT program is a revision of the MIN program, and it completes the SORT so that the list is sorted and outputted from the least to the greatest. In line 300 of the SORT program, a new concept is introduced. The string array (INPUT R$) is introduced as a convenience to allow the student to control the speed of the SORT and to watch as the list is sorted. The INPUT R$ entry allows the student to watch one line of the sort exchange and when the RETURN key (R$ = "RETURN") is pressed, the next line of the exchange can be viewed. Remove INPUT R$ and the SORT moves along at computer speed. String arrays will be discussed in the next lesson.

Type in the MIN program, RUN, and compare with the MIN-MAX program.

```
100   REM*PROGRAM TO SELECT MIN NUMBER
110   REM*FROM A LIST OF N NUMBERS
120   INPUT "HOW MANY NUMBERS", N : DIM L(N)
130   FOR K = 1 TO N
140   PRINT "L(";K;")=";
150   INPUT L(K)
160   NEXT K : T = 1
170   PRINT "THIS IS THE ORIGINAL LIST" : PRINT
180   FOR J = 1 TO N : TAB T
190   PRINT "L(";J;")=";L(J); : T = T + 10 : IF T<33 THEN 200 : PRINT :
      PRINT : T = 1
200   NEXT J : IF T = 1 THEN 210 : PRINT : PRINT
210   FOR T = 1 TO N−1 : MNS = T : F = T + 1
220   FOR J = F TO N
230   IF L(J)<L(MNS) THEN MNS = J
240   NEXT J
250   J = L(T) : L(T) = L(MNS) : L(MNS) = J
260   PRINT "MIN =";L(T) : PRINT
270   PRINT "L(";T;") AND L(";MNS;") WERE EXCHANGED" : PRINT
280   F = 1 : FOR J = 1 TO N : TAB F
290   PRINT "L(";J;")=";L(J) : F = F + 10 : IF F<33 THEN 300 : PRINT :
      PRINT : F = 1
300   NEXT J  : INPUT R$ : NEXT T
999   END
RUN
HOW MANY NUMBERS? 4
L(1) = ?5
L(2) = ?8
L(3) = ?3
L(4) = ?1
HERE IS THE ORIGINAL LIST
```

```
L(1) = 5  L(2) = 8  L(3) = 3  L(4) = 1
MIN = 1
L(1) AND L(4) WERE EXCHANGED
L(1) = 1  L(2) = 8  L(3) = 3  L(4) = 5
```

Lines 100 through 160 input the amount of numbers in the list, DIMension memory, and input the numbers in the list. Line 170 prints out the heading for the list of numbers. Then, line 180 sets the loop to print the numbers in the list. The TAB T (T = 1, line 160) tabulates the position of the number to be printed in column number 1. Line 190 prints the value of the number in the memory location whose label is L(J). Entry T = T + 10 spaces each printout 10 spaces from the previous L(J) printout. Then, entry IF T<33 THEN 200 checks to see if T is less than 33. If the answer is "no," another L(J) is printed. If the answer is "yes" (T<33), the program branches to line 200—the NEXT J. The first PRINT closes out the line. The second PRINT causes a line to be skipped, and T is set to 1 to prepare the TAB to PRINT the next L(J) in the first column of the next line. Line 200 (NEXT J) executes the loop until it reaches N numbers and the list outputted.

Line 210 begins T = 1. In this case, the variable T is unrelated to the T = 1 in line 160 that caused TAB T to print in column number 1. The same variable may be used for different functions throughout the program. Entry T = 1 is used in relation to line 250, in order to exchange values in the list, so that it can be printed least to greatest. This will be explained in the SORT program that follows the MIN program. Entry T = 1 sets the value of the subscript at which the MIN number is to be placed. For this example, the top of the list is L(T), or since T = 1, L(1). This is a replacement statement that places the subscript value into T. Remember, the subscripted variable where the MIN is found is L(MNS). Since T = 1 and we now have MNS = T, the value of 1 is placed in the subscript MNS. The first comparison assumes the MIN number is in L(1)—the L(MNS) location. The subscript MNS where the MIN number is to be found is kept so the list can be modified; in other words, we need to know where the MIN is, not what the MIN is, in order to put it at the top of the list.

The final statement in line 210 is F = T + 1. This is a variation of F = a constant (F = 2). This is used to demonstrate flexibility of programming where constants are fixed and variables change within a loop. It is useful in PRINT and TAB statements. The entry F = 2 could have been used just as well in this statement to prepare for line 220.

Line 220 is FOR J = F TO N (this is the same as FOR J = 2 TO N). The first value of the list was placed in L(1). Since it is unnecessary to compare L(MNS) to L(1), the loop begins with the second number in the list. The program statements in line 210 cause the microcomputer to assume that the MIN is the first number in the list.

Line 230 states IF L(J) < L(MNS) THEN MIN = J. If L(J) is less than the previous MIN value found in L(MNS), then the value of the subscript J is stored in the minimum subscript MNS. J and MNS are subscripts, not the value of the numbers in the list. Line 230 keeps track of the subscript value where the MIN number can be found in the list.

Line 240 NEXT J finishes the loop. Line 250 will place the MIN number at the top of the list for ease of reference, and will be used and explained in detail in the SORT program.

Line 260 prints out the minimum value and is printed by using the contents whose memory label is L(MNS). The PRINT causes a line space between the last print and the next print.

Line 270 educates the student so that the shift can be viewed and the subscripts show where the shift takes place.

Line 280 entry F = 1 is used to set the TAB F to column number 1, and the loop statement FOR J = 1 TO N prepares to output the list.

Line 290 prints the subscript and the value of the number in the subscript. The statement F = F + 10 spaces (advances) to print the next subscripted variable and the number. IF F<33 is false (no), the outputted line is closed out, a line is skipped, and F = 1 is reset to print in column number 1. IF F<33 is true (yes), it branches to the NEXT J and continues through the loop.

A SORT PROGRAM

The SORT program is a final progression in the series. The logical learning process is MIN-MAX first, MIN second, and SORT third.

The MIN program was written with extra program lines in it. Thus, the SORT program has only three statements to change so that the list of N numbers can be sorted and printed from "least" to "greatest."

A FOR   NEXT loop is added to make passes through the list and exchange the numbers.

(SORT)	210	FOR T = 1 TO N−1 : MNS = T : F = T + 1
(MIN)	210	T = 1 : MNS = T : F = T + 1
(SORT)	300	NEXT J : INPUT R$: NEXT T
(MIN)	300	NEXT J

SORT line 210 lists FOR T = 1 TO N−1. Since there are four numbers in the list, it is necessary to make only three passes through the list. The number of passes in the list is N−1. The INPUT R$ entry on line 300 is a convenience entry that is inserted in the program so

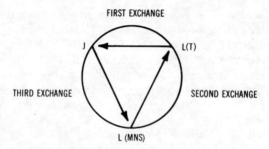

Fig. 14-2. Symbolic representation of an exchange in a SORT program.

the user can control the speed of the sort. By pressing RETURN and releasing it, the user can control the speed at which the program RUNs. R$ is a new concept (string arrays will be discussed in the next lesson).

Now, to line 250 which lists J = L(T) : L(T) = L(MNS : L(MNS) = J. The list in the SORT program is 9 3 6 1. L(T) is the position in the list where the MIN is to be placed. L(MNS) is the value of the minimum subscripted variable. J is a temporary storage location.

$$L(1) = 9$$
$$L(2) = 3$$
$$L(3) = 6$$
$$L(4) = 1$$

The circle, shown in Fig. 14-2, is a symbolic representation that is used for demonstration purposes only. In the first pass, L(T) is L(1).

The purpose of the exchange is to change the value contained in L(T) with the value contained in L(MNS) (the minimum value in the list), and vice-versa. To accomplish this, a temporary storage location J is required in memory. On the first pass, the objective is to exchange L(1) with L(4). T = 1, so L(T) = L(1) because the FOR T = 1 TO N−1 loop starts at 1 (FOR T = 1) and the L(MNS) for the pass is in L(4). This is shown in Table 14-1, as are the values during the second and third passes.

There is no fourth pass since the loop FOR T = 1 TO N−1 executes N−1 times, or 3 times, since the N amount of numbers in the list is 4. The list is sorted and the output is 1 3 6 9. On the first execution of loop FOR T = 1 TO N−1, the MIN number is in L(1). On the second execution of the loop, the second MIN number is placed in L(2). In this case, the second MIN number was already in L(2). On the third execution of the loop, the third MIN number was placed in L(3).

Table 14-1. Table of Passes and Exchanges

		J	L(T)	L(MNS)	
ORIGINAL			9	1	
First Pass	First Exchange	9	9	1	J = L(T)
	Second Exchange	9	1	1	L(T) = L(MNS)
	Third Exchange	1	1	9	L(MNS) = J
Second Pass	First Exchange	3	3	3	J = L(T)
	Second Exchange	3	3	3	L(T) = L(MNS)
	Third Exchange	3	3	3	L(MNS) = J
Third Pass	First Exchange	6	6	6	J = L(T)
	Second Exchange	6	6	6	L(T) = L(MNS)
	Third Exchange	6	6	6	L(MNS) = J
		9	9	9	

The data remains the same after the first exchange because the list was in proper order from "least" to "greatest" after the first pass. The complete SORT program and RUN follows.

```
100  REM*PROGRAM TO SORT LIST
110  REM*FROM LEAST TO GREATEST
120  INPUT "HOW MANY NUMBERS", N : DIM L(N)
130  FOR K = 1 TO N
140  PRINT "L(";K;")=";
150  INPUT L(K)
160  NEXT K : T = 1
170  PRINT "THIS IS THE ORIGINAL LIST" : PRINT
180  FOR J = 1 TO N : TAB T
190  PRINT "L(";J;")=";L(J) : T = T + 10 : IF T<33 THEN 200 : PRINT :
     PRINT : T = 1
200  NEXT J : IF T = 1 THEN 210 : PRINT : PRINT
210  FOR T = 1 TO N−1 : MNS = T : F = T + 1
220  FOR J = F TO N
230  IF L(J)<L(MNS) THEN MNS = J
240  NEXT J : PRINT : IF MNS = T THEN 255
250  J = L(T) : L(T) = L(MNS) : L(MNS) = J
255  NEXT T
260  PRINT "MIN = ";L(T) : PRINT
270  PRINT "L(";T;") AND L(";MNS;") WERE EXCHANGED" : PRINT
280  F = 1 : FOR J = 1 TO N : TAB F
290  PRINT "L(";J;")=";L(J); : F = F + 10 : IF F<33 THEN 300 : PRINT :
     PRINT : F = 1
300  NEXT J : INPUT R$ : NEXT T
999  END
RUN
HOW MANY NUMBERS? 4
L(1) = 9
L(2) = 3
L(3) = 6
L(4) = 1
THIS IS THE ORIGINAL LIST
```

```
L(1) = 9  L(2) = 3  L(3) = 6  L(4) = 1
MIN = 1
L(1) AND L(4) WERE EXCHANGED
L(1) = 1  L(2) = 3  L(3) = 6  L(4) = 9
(PRESS RETURN)
MIN = 3
L(2) AND L(2) WERE EXCHANGED
L(1) = 1  L(2) = 3  L(3) = 6  L(4) = 9
(PRESS RETURN)
MIN = 6
L(3) AND L(3) WERE EXCHANGED
L(1) = 1  L(2) = 3  L(3) = 6  L(4) = 9
```

EXERCISES

1. Define ten new words from your computer dictionary.

2. Practice and study the MIN-MAX, MIN, and SORT programs until you can understand the logic completely. As a test, write a MIN-MAX, a MIN, and a SORT program using different variables to determine that you understand the programs.

LESSON 15

Strings and GOSUB

After completion of this lesson, you should be able to:

1. Write programs using strings.

VOCABULARY

GOSUB—causes a branch to BASIC subroutine starting at the legal line number specified by the expression.

Literal—a sequence of characters. A string is a literal enclosed in quotation marks.

Null string—contains zero characters. Uses the RETURN key to continue the program.

String—is any set of characters that is not treated as a number but is to be otherwise manipulated by the microcomputer. The characters are referred to as alphanumeric, since alpha and numeric characters and most of the other symbols produced by the terminal are permitted. A sequence of characters enclosed in quotation marks.

EXAMPLE OF A STRING

Strings are used primarily for storing names and addresses. Previously, the use of alphanumeric characters was limited to the use of strings in a PRINT statement.

```
10   PRINT "THIS IS THE USA"
```

A string variable ends with a "$" sign and the literal, or sequence of characters, is enclosed in quotation marks, as shown in the following example:

```
10    A$ = "THIS IS THE USA"
```

A string may contain from 0 (zero) to 255 characters. The string variable may be any variable name followed by a dollar sign ($). It is pronounced A-dollar, or A-string. The following are examples of strings:

A$ ABCDEFG$ NAME$ JOHN$

The string, like the subscripted variable, must use a DIM(dimension) statement to reserve specific memory.

```
10    DIM A$(60)
```

To determine the length of a string, the following command is used to print out the number of characters in the string:

```
PRINT LEN (A$)
```

Type in the following program and RUN it.

```
10    DIM A$(60)
20    A$ = "JOHN DOE 2200 MAIN ST. ANYTOWN, USA 00000"
30    PRINT A$ : PRINT
40    PRINT A$(1,8) : PRINT
50    PRINT A$(10,23) : PRINT
60    PRINT A$(25,43)
99 END
RUN
JOHN DOE 2200 MAIN ST. ANYTOWN, USA 00000
JOHN DOE
2200 MAIN ST.
ANYTOWN, USA 00000
```

Line 20 establishes the literal, in quotes, using the relational operator to shift the value of the string to the A$.

Line 30 prints the string by using the statement PRINT A$.

Line 40 uses a method to output the first through the eighth characters in the string. Line 40 uses subscripts to print part of the string A$(1,8). In this case, the first through the eighth characters in A$ are outputted when the program is RUN, and that output is the name "JOHN DOE." The Apple II using Integer BASIC allows single subscripted strings such as A$(I), and double subscripted strings such as A$(I,J). The I is the Ith element of the string, while I,J are the Ith through the Jth elements of the string. The advantage of the subscripted string array is that any part or parts of the array can be dealt with directly. Integer BASIC (for the Apple II) does not allow IF   THEN statements to compare strings using relational operators. This deficiency can be overcome, however. (See the Appendix for the explanation of the method.) Note that if line 40 had used PRINT A$(0,8), a *** STRING ERR would have occurred because 0 (zero) is an illegal value.

Line 50 outputs the eleventh through the twenty-third characters which are "2200 MAIN ST." Line 60 outputs the twenty-sixth through the forty-fourth characters which are "ANYTOWN, USA 00000." In this simple manner, any part of a string may be outputted.

To change the program, type in the following line.

```
20   INPUT A$
```

Now, you can type in your name and address. Does it output correctly? Probably not, unless your name is the same number of characters as "JOHN DOE." In the A$(1,8) statement, A$ numbers are specific and output only the first through the eighth characters. To be of value, the program must be flexible enough so any number of characters in the name and address will be accepted as input and the output will be in a standard usable form. To achieve this flexibility, a delimiter (;) is used after the name of the person and, again, after the street number and name. As a step toward that flexible formula, an inflexible formula is demonstrated in the following program.

```
10   DIM A$(60)
20   A$ = "JOHN DOE;2200 MAIN ST.;ANYTOWN, USA 00000"
30   N = 9 : A1 = 23 : L = LEN(A$)
40   PRINT A$ : PRINT
50   PRINT A$(1,N−1) : PRINT
60   PRINT A$(N+1,A1−1) : PRINT
70   PRINT A$(A1+1,L)
99   END
RUN
JOHN DOE;2200 MAIN ST.;ANYTOWN, USA 00000
JOHN DOE
2200 MAIN ST.
ANYTOWN, USA 00000
(A$ = "JOHN DOE;2200 MAIN ST.;ANYTOWN, USA 00000")
```

The semicolon (;) is used as a delimiter to separate the fields in the A$ statement. The variables locate the delimiters at the end of each field. No spaces are left between the contents of the field and the delimiter. The following is an explanation of the expressions used in the program.

$N = 9$	N = variable of the delimiter at the end of the first field. Nine (9) is the column the delimiter occupies.
$A1 = 23$	A1 = variable of the delimiter at the end of the second field. Twenty-three (23) is the column the delimiter occupies.
$L = LEN(A\$)$	L points to the end of the third field. The column that L occupies is deter-

mined by the length of the City, State, and Zip Code.

The subscripted arrays for lines 1 through 3 are as shown in the following list. They are further explained in Table 15-1.

Line 1   A\$(1,N−1)
Line 2   A\$(N+1,A1−1)
Line 3   A\$(A1+1,L)

Table 15-1. Table Showing Where Lines Start and End

LINE	START	SYMBOL	END	SYMBOL
1	A\$(1,—)	1	Before first delimiter	N−1
2	After first delimiter	N+1	Before second delimiter	A1−1
3	After second delimiter	A1+1	Length of string	L

In this sequence of learning events, the first subscripted array has constants within the parenthesis of A\$(1,8) that printed out the first through the eighth characters in the string. The second type of subscripted array has a constant and a variable with a fixed value when used in relation to the delimiter A\$(1,N−1) and a fixed A\$ input. The following program has variable length input and a delimiter that is determined by the variable input A\$(1, D1C−1). This program, with variable length input and decisions that can check the input errors, is bringing you closer to the real world of programming.

Development of a complicated program is a detailed, exacting, and thought-provoking process. Not all of the author's thoughts can be written on paper. The following program is presented in the detailed manner that it was developed, showing the logical lines it followed. The final program varies from the outline flowchart and this is a feature that shows a progressively changing thought. For the benefit of the student, the initial flowcharts were not changed to conform to the finished program. The differences shown from one step to the next are to emphasize how development occurs.

1. Outline of program development.
   A. What is the problem?
   B. Detailed input format.
   C. Detailed output format.
   D. Outline flowchart.
   E. Assignment of variables.
   F. Start and end of lines.
   G. Assignment of line lengths.

H. Error checking.
- (1) Number of delimiters.
- (2) Length of lines.
  - (a) Length of line 1.
  - (b) Length of line 2.
  - (c) Length of line 3.

I. Write error-checking section of flowchart outline.
J. Final flowchart.
K. Write program.
L. Debug and modify program.
M. Final program.

(The explanations and details of the logic that is used follow the same number coding as the preceding outline.)

1A

What is the problem? The problem is to input three lines of variable length that are separated by a delimiter (;) in order to allow any length of name, street number and street name, and city, state, and zip code up to 255 characters.

1B

What is the detailed input format? It is the line of input A$. It is:

JOHN DOE;2200 MAIN ST.;ANYTOWN, USA   00000

1C

What is the detailed output format? It is:

JOHN DOE
2200 MAIN ST.
ANYTOWN, USA   00000

1D

What is an outline flowchart? An outline flowchart is a step in the program development. Like the man said, "You start at the beginning and you end at the end." The middle is developed according to logic and program needs. Fig. 15-1 shows the outline flowchart that is used in this series.

1E

What determines the assignment of variables? The variables used the logic that a delimiter (D) was used after line (1) to close the line, thus D1C. The $L = LEN(A\$)$ was the delimiter to be used at the end of line 3. The following list shows the assignment of expressions.

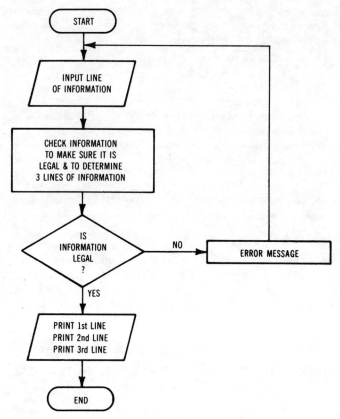

Fig. 15-1. Flowchart for the program development outline.

1 (first column)	Beginning of line 1.
D1C	Points to the delimiter at the end of line 1.
D1C−1	End of line 1.
D1C+1	Beginning of line 2.
D2C	Points to the delimiter at the end of line 2.
D2C−1	End of line 2.
D2C+1	Beginning of line 3.
L	End of line 3.
ERR	Variable that is assigned a value when an input error has occurred, and the value is used to print the type of error.
J − (J,J)	Loop variable or subscript variable (of a string).
Kn	Constant.

1F

Determine the start and end of lines. Once the delimiter variables are assigned, they are placed at the start and end of the lines. Table 15-2 further explains their placement.

Line 1 $A\$(1,D1C \pm K1)$
Line 2 $A\$(D1C \pm K2,D2C \pm K3)$
Line 3 $A\$(D2C \pm K4,L)$

Table 15-2. Table Showing Where Lines Start and End

LINE	START	SYMBOL	END	SYMBOL
1	Beginning of column 1	$A\$(1,-)$	Before first delimiter	$D1C-1$
2	After first delimiter	$D1C+1$	Before second delimiter	$D2C-1$
3	After second delimiter	$D2C+1$	Length of string	L

1G

Determine the assignment of line lengths. The assignment of line lengths is the logical progression once the start and end of the lines are determined. The input is as shown in Fig. 15-2 and it is explained by the variables, as follows:

Line 1 $A\$(1,D1C-1)$
Line 2 $A\$(D1C+1,D2C-1)$
Line 3 $A\$(D2C+1,L)$

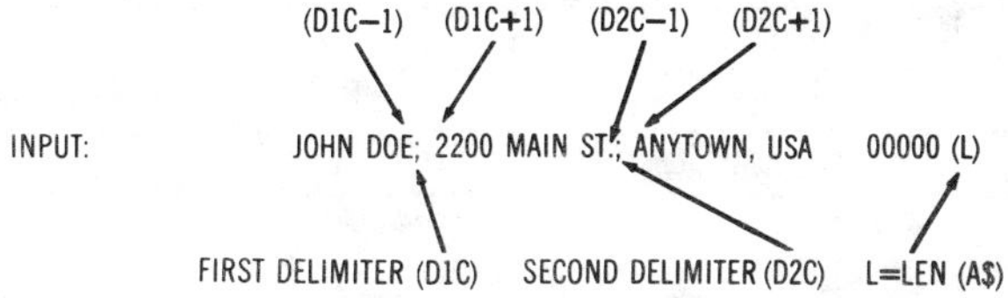

INPUT: JOHN DOE; 2200 MAIN ST., ANYTOWN, USA   00000 (L)

(D1C−1) (D1C+1) (D2C−1) (D2C+1)

FIRST DELIMITER (D1C)   SECOND DELIMITER (D2C)   L=LEN (A$)

Fig. 15-2. Input used to determine line lengths.

1H

An examination of error checking shows that for a program to be effective and efficient, those situations that will interrupt the flow must be eliminated. Some illegal conditions that will interrupt program flow are:

1. Delimiters if there are not exactly two (2).
2. If the length of the line is not correct.
   A. Length of line 1 = 0.

B. Length of line 2 = 0.
C. Length of line 3 = 0.

First, we will examine the number of delimiters. The input format specifies two, and only two, delimiters. If there are any more or any less than two delimiters, the input is illegal.

Table 15-3. Check for the Number of Delimiters

DELIMITER NBR.	TEST SHOWS	DECISION STATEMENT
0	Illegal	D1C>L
1	Illegal	D2C>L
2	Legal	
3	Illegal	FOR J = D2C+1 TO L IF A$(J,J) = ";" NEXT J

Then, the length of the lines must be checked. There are three lines of input separated by delimiters. If any or all of these lines are zero length, the input is incorrect.

Line 1 = 0   ;2200 MAIN ST.;ANYTOWN, USA 00000(L)
Line 2 = 0   JOHN DOE;;ANYTOWN, USA 00000(L)
Line 3 = 0   JOHN DOE;2200 MAIN ST.;(L)

Table 15-4. Error Check for Line Length

LINE	CONDITION	DECISION	STATEMENT IS
1	;MAIN;USA	D1C = 1	Illegal
2	DOE;;USA	D1C+1=D2C	Illegal
3	DOE;MAIN;(L)	L = D2C	Illegal

11

Write the error-checking section of the outline flowchart. Once the legal and illegal values relating to error checking have been determined, they must be prepared for the final flowchart. The details of the error-checking section of the flowchart are shown in Fig. 15-3.

In a flowchart with no error-checking statement (our first example), the flowchart statements are:

```
L = LEN(A$)
D1C = 0
D1C = D1C + 1
IF A$(D1C,D1C) = ";"
D2C = D1C
```

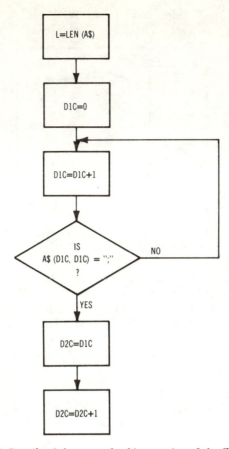

Fig. 15-3. Details of the error-checking section of the flowchart.

If the answer to the statement of IF A\$(D1C,D1C) = ";" is a NO, the program loops back to D1C = D1C + 1. If there are no delimiters separating the name and address fields in "DOE MAIN USA" A\$ string, the D1C = D1C + 1 loop executes until D1C is greater than L. When D1C is greater than L, the computer prints *** STRING ERR, because you are telling the machine to compare a nonexistent character to ";". This is shown by line 13 of Table 15-5.

Next, we will examine a flowchart with an error-checking statement. It is as follows:

```
L = LEN(A$)
D1C = 0
D1C = D1C + 1
IS D1C > L ? IF YES, PRINT "ILLEGAL INPUT" : GOTO INPUT
IS A$(D1C,D1C) = ";" ?
```

Table 15-5. Input With No Error-Checking Statement

DOE MAIN USA	
D1C	A$(D1C,D1C)
1	D
2	O
3	E
4	
5	M
6	A
7	I
8	N
9	
10	U
11	S
12	A
13	*** STRING ERR

When the error-checking statement IF D1C > L is placed in the flowchart, it checks to see if a delimiter is in the input information. The IF D1C > L statement processes the information and if no delimiter is present, it branches to a PRINT "ILLEGAL INPUT" and, then, to a GOTO INPUT statement. Otherwise, the program proceeds to process. A NO answer to the string variable will cause a loop back to D1C = D1C + 1.

1J

The final flowchart is shown in Fig. 15-4. This final flowchart is an incorporation of all the details, charts, ideas, and logic up to this point. The final flowchart should be diagrammed and written so that very few changes will be needed to produce the written program.

Final Steps

The final three steps are 1K, 1L, and 1M, which specify the need to write, debug, and modify the program. Now that the program has been written, debugged, modified, and RUN, it should be finished. However, most programmers are perpetual students, tinkerers, and perfectionists. They will usually seek modifications to do the job better. This is the total idea to life and programming.

THE PROGRAM

The completed program is as follows:

```
100   REM*PRINT NAME & ADDRESS &
110   REM*CHECK FOR INPUT ERRORS
```

```
120   DIM A$(255), Q$(1)
130   PRINT "INPUT 'NAME;ADDRESS;CITY,STATE, ZIP'"
140   INPUT "?",A$
150   L = LEN(A$)
160   D1C = 0
170   D1C = D1C + 1
180   IF D1C < = L THEN 190 : ERR = 0 : GOSUB 390 : GOTO 130
190   IF A$(D1C,D1C) # ";" THEN 170
200   IF D1C # 1 THEN 220
210   ERR = 1 : GOSUB 390 : GOTO 130
220   D2C = D1C
230   D2C = D2C + 1
240   IF D2C < = L THEN 250 : ERR = 2 : GOSUB 390 : GOTO 130
250   IF A$(D2C,D2C) # ";" THEN 230
260   IF D1C + 1 < D2C THEN 280
270   ERR = 3 : GOSUB 390 : GOTO 130
280   IF D2C < L THEN 300
290   ERR = 4 : GOSUB 390 : GOTO 130
300   FOR J = D2C + 1 TO L
310   IF A$(J,J) # ";" THEN 320 : ERR = 5 : GOSUB 390 : GOTO 130
320   NEXT J
330   PRINT A$(1, D1C-1) : PRINT
340   PRINT A$(D1C+1,D2C−1) : PRINT
350   PRINT A$(D2C+1,L) : PRINT
360   INPUT "MORE INPUT (Y OR N)" ,Q$
370   IF Q$ = "N" THEN 380 : GOTO 130
380   END
390   PRINT "ILLEGAL INPUT" : PRINT A$
400   GOTO 410 + ERR*10
410   PRINT "NO DELIMITER IN STRING" : RETURN
420   PRINT "LINE 1 IS ZERO LENGTH" : RETURN
430   PRINT "ONLY 1 DELIMITER IN STRING" : RETURN
440   PRINT "LINE 2 IS ZERO LENGTH" : RETURN
450   PRINT "LINE 3 IS ZERO LENGTH" : RETURN
460   PRINT "MORE THAN 2 DELIMITERS IN STRING" : RETURN
RUN
INPUT 'NAME;ADDRESS;CITY, STATE, ZIP'
?JOHN DOE;2200 MAIN ST.;ANYTOWN, USA 00000
JOHN DOE
2200 MAIN ST.
ANYTOWN, USA 00000
MORE INPUT (Y OR N)
INPUT 'NAME;ADDRESS;CITY, STATE, ZIP'
?JOHN DOE 2200 MAIN ST. ANYTOWN, USA 00000
ILLEGAL INPUT
NO DELIMITER IN STRING
INPUT 'NAME;ADDRESS;CITY, STATE, ZIP'
?JOHN DOE;2200 MAIN ST.ANYTOWN, USA 00000
ILLEGAL INPUT
ONLY 1 DELIMITER IN STRING
INPUT 'NAME;ADDRESS;CITY, STATE, ZIP'
?JOHN DOE;2200 MAIN ST.;ANYTOWN, USA 00000;
ILLEGAL INPUT
MORE THAN 2 DELIMITERS IN STRING
INPUT 'NAME;ADDRESS;CITY, STATE, ZIP'
```

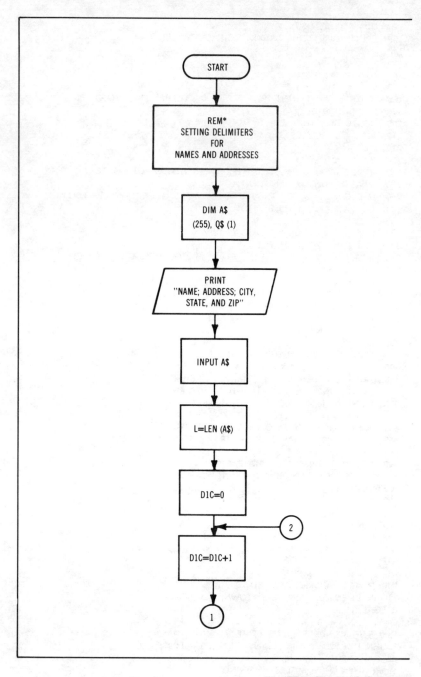

Fig. 15-4. The final flowchart

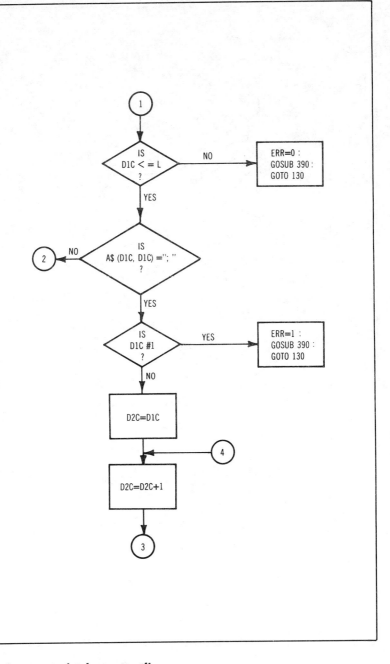

for the program development outline.

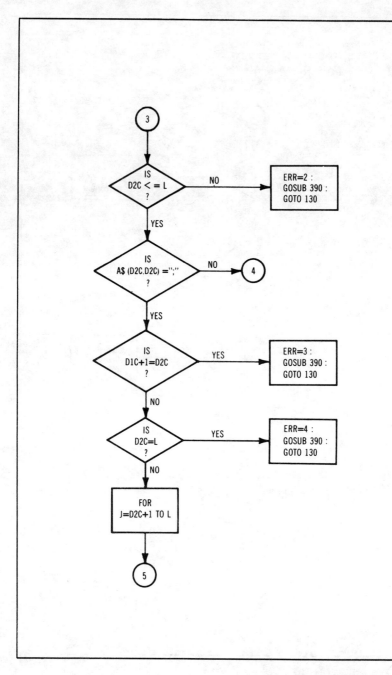

Fig. 15-4. Cont. The final flowchart

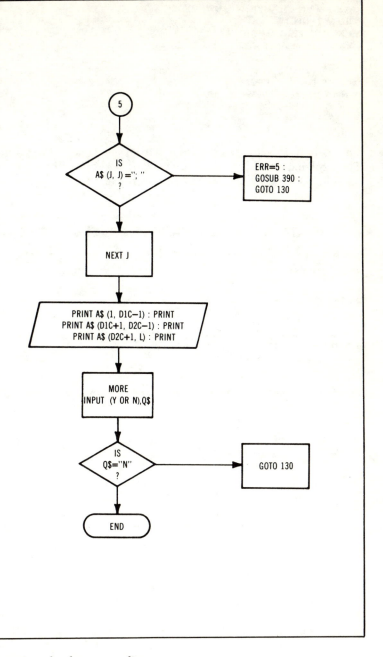

for the program development outline.

```
;2200 MAIN ST.;ANYTOWN, USA 00000
ILLEGAL INPUT
LINE 1 IS ZERO LENGTH
INPUT 'NAME;ADDRESS;CITY, STATE, ZIP'
?JOHN DOE;;ANYTOWN, USA   00000
ILLEGAL INPUT
LINE 2 IS ZERO LENGTH
INPUT 'NAME;ADDRESS;CITY, STATE, ZIP'
?JOHN DOE;2200 MAIN ST;
ILLEGAL INPUT
LINE 3 IS ZERO LENGTH
```

This is how the logic is developed from conception to completion. The explanation of line numbers may be repetitious but it may also be helpful. The decision statements were changed for programming efficiency according to the three rules of efficient programming.

CHANGES FOR EFFICIENT PROGRAMMING

There are several ways to write a program and, sometimes, just a slight change might make it more efficient. For example, four original variables might be written to determine some maximum values, as follows:

```
IF D1C > L THEN DO 2 THINGS
IF D1C = 1 THEN DO 2 THINGS
IF D1C+1 > D2C THEN DO 2 THINGS
IF D2C > L THEN DO 2 THINGS
```

However, if the program was rewritten to determine the lesser amount of a quantity, it is possible that the final program variables would require less memory to operate, as follows:

```
IF D1C < = L THEN DO 1 THING
IF D1C # 1 THEN DO 1 THING
IF D1C+1 < D2C THEN DO 1 THING
IF D2C < L THEN DO 1 THING
```

The line 120 statement DIM A$(255), Q$(1) sets reserved memory to the maximum limit allowed by the APPLE II. Q$(1) reserves memory for a "Y" (yes) or "N" (no) answer to line 360, thus allowing a request for more input or a request to end the program. Line 130 indicates the exact manner in which information is to be input. No spaces should be left between fields of input and delimiters. Line 140 allows A$ input into the program. Line 150 statement of L = LEN (A$) is a programming convenience. L is much easier to type than LEN (A$). Line 160 initializes the variable of the first delimiter to zero. Line 170 statement D1C = D1C + 1 begins the loop that checks the alphanumeric characters before the first delimiter. The loop is executed until the computer locates D1C and stores the position at the end of the name field in memory for further use.

Line 180 is a decision statement of IF D1C < = L THEN 190. This checks to see if there is a delimiter at the end of the first name field and before the end of the length of the string. This is the first error check. If there is no delimiter, ERR = 0 is printed. The program branches to GOSUB 390 and prints ILLEGAL INPUT. NO DELIMITER IN STRING. This tells the input operator where the error has occurred. If there is a delimiter after the name field (line 1 of input), the program defaults to line 190.

Line 190 is the end of the loop to check for the delimiter. If IF A$(J,J) is not equal to ";" (the delimiter), the loop branches to increment D1C = D1C + 1 in line 170, and executes until a delimiter is encountered.

Line 200 statement of IF D1C # 1 THEN 220 branches the program to line 220, where the statement is D2C = D1C. The value of D1C is placed in D2C to keep track of the name spaces from the last line, and adds the first name spaces to the beginning of line 2 of input. If D1C is equal to 1, it means the delimiter is in column 1 of the name field.

Lines 200 to 290 are related directly to the error input table (Table 15-6), and to the decision statement sections of Tables 15-3 and 15-4.

Table 15-6. Error Input Table

ERROR	GOTO		ERR*10	LINE
0	410	+	0 * 10	410
1	410	+	1 * 10	420
2	410	+	2 * 10	430
3	410	+	3 * 10	440
4	410	+	4 * 10	450
5	410	+	5 * 10	460

Line 300 is a decision loop (FOR J = D2C + 1 TO L) that is used to check the CITY, STATE, ZIP field to determine if there are delimiters between D2C and the end of A$. Line 300 is used in conjunction with line 310 statement of IF A$(J,J) # ";" THEN 320 to cause a branch to line 320. The line 320 statement of NEXT J causes the loop to continue executing.

Lines 330, 340, and 350 print the specific A$ fields, namely, the Name, the Street Number and Name, and the City, State, and Zip Code.

Line 360 statement of INPUT "MORE INPUT (Y OR N)" ,Q$ allows the user to press "Y" (yes) to input more data or press "N" (no) to end the program. Q$(1) was DIMensioned in line 120. The

107

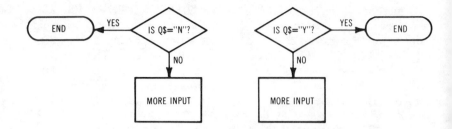

ENTERED	RESULT	RESULT
N (NO)	END	END
Y (YES)	MORE INPUT	MORE INPUT
ANYTHING ELSE	MORE INPUT	END

Fig. 15-5. The logic diagram of IF Q$ = "N" THEN END.

"Y" or "N" is a convenient way for the user to either input more data or end the program.

The logic of the IF Q$ = "N" THEN 380 : GOTO 130 statement shown on line 370 is detailed in Fig. 15-5. Fig. 15-5 also includes the line 380 statement of END. When the statement IF Q$ = "N" is used, the chances are an untrained operator will get a 33% more satisfactory result than with the statement IF Q$ = "Y". On programs where a yes or no answer is critical, the program can be written so that the decision statement will allow only a yes or no answer, and will disallow any other input.

Subroutines are placed after the main program and are shown in lines 390 through 460. The main body of the program ENDs at line 380. However, the GOSUB 390 subroutine within the main body of the program causes a branch to line 390 to print out "ILLEGAL INPUT" and then default to line 400.

The line 400 statement of GOTO 410 + ERR*10 causes the proper error message to be printed, as shown in Table 15-6.

There are many programs that can input names and addresses but this program incorporates most of the features necessary to check input errors. Programs should solve problems and output in the proper format, but the program should also be self-checking at the time of input. Program error checking is similar to the *** STRING ERR in Integer BASIC. The error should be detected and corrected almost immediately for maximum efficiency.

The following program demonstrates how a name and address can be input with little or no error checking. This program is about one-third as long as the previous program and will do the same job IF the input is correct.

```
0    DIM A$(255)
10   INPUT "NAME ?",A$
20   L = LEN (A$) : D1C = L + 1 : A$(D1C) = ";"
30   INPUT "STREET ADDRESS ?" ,A$(D1C + 1)
40   L = LEN (A$) : D2C = L + 1 : A$(D2C) = ";"
50   INPUT "CITY, STATE, ZIP ?" , A$(D2C + 1)
60   L = LEN (A$)
70   PRINT A$(1, D1C − 1) : PRINT
80   PRINT A$(D1C + 1, D2C − 1) : PRINT
90   PRINT A$(D2C + 1, L) : PRINT
100  END
RUN
NAME?JOHN DOE
STREET ADDRESS?2200 MAIN ST.
CITY, STATE, ZIP?ANYTOWN, USA   00000
JOHN DOE
2200 MAIN ST.
ANYTOWN, USA   00000
```

EXERCISES

1. Define ten new words from your computer dictionary.

2. Rewrite the name and address program using new variables of your own choosing.

LESSON 16

Functions

After completion of this lesson, you should be able to:

1. Program using functions.

VOCABULARY

ABS—gives the absolute value of the expression.

ASC—gives the ASCII value of the character. ASCII is an acronym for American Standard Code for Information Interchange.

RND—gives a random number.

SCRN—gives a color (number between 0 and 15) of the screen at a horizontal and a vertical location.

SGN—gives the sign of the expression, i.e., −1 if expression is negative, zero if the expression is zero, and +1 if the expression is positive.

EXAMPLE PROGRAMS

Two programs are presented in this lesson. One program simply lists the functions available in Integer BASIC (for the Apple II) and the RUN presents the results. The second program presents a detailed usage of the RND function. It shows a program that will shuffle a deck of cards. Type in the following program so as to demonstrate the functions.

```
100   REM*PROGRAM TO DEMONSTRATE
110   REM*FUNCTIONS
120   M = −4 : N = 7 : O = 4
```

```
130    PRINT ABS(M) : PRINT
140    PRINT ASC("X") : PRINT
150    PRINT ASC("X")  MOD 128 : PRINT
160    PRINT SCRN(N,O) : PRINT
170    PRINT SGN(M) : PRINT
180    PRINT SGN(N) : PRINT
190    PRINT RND(6) + 1 : PRINT
200    FOR J = 1 TO 5
210    PRINT RND(J) + 1,
220    NEXT J : PRINT
230    END
RUN
4                          (ABS value of −4)
216                        (ASC value of X)
88                         (ASC value of X MOD 128)
−1                         (SGN of −4 is −1 since it is negative)
1                          (SGN of +7 is 1 since it is positive)
3                          (RND number of 6)
1    2    1    2    4      (RND numbers from 1 to 5)
0                          (SCRN color at N,O is zero)
```

While the program is self-explanatory, the MOD concept has not been discussed. In Integer BASIC, when a number is divided by another number, the results are truncated.

$$23/4 = 5$$

To overcome this deficiency of not giving a remainder, the MOD function is used.

Step No. 1   PRINT 23/4
5   (truncated results)
Step No. 2   23 MOD 4
3   (remainder)

The following program will demonstrate the RND function:

```
S$ = SUIT  F$ = FACE CARD  S = SHUFFLE  V = VALUE OF THE CARD

100    REM*DEMONSTRATE RND FUNCTION
110    REM*SHUFFLE A DECK OF CARDS
120    DIM D(52), S$(4), F$(4), Q$(1) : CALL −936
130    S$ = "SHCD" : F$ = "JQKA"
140    FOR J = 1 TO 52
150    D(J) = J − 1 : NEXT J
160    PRINT "YOU ARE STARTING WITH A FRESH DECK"
165    PRINT "HOW MANY TIMES DO YOU WANT IT" : INPUT "SHUFFLED",S
170    IF S > = 0 THEN 190
180    PRINT "COME NOW SIR, WE'LL HAVE NO JOKES" : PRINT "AT THIS TABLE"
       : GOTO 160
190    IF S<8 THEN 220
200    PRINT "PROBABILITY THEORY SHOWS THAT BETWEEN" : PRINT "3 AND 8
       SHUFFLES SHOULD BE SUFFICIENT"
210    INPUT "ENTER 'T' TO TRY AGAIN",Q$ : IF Q$ = "T" THEN 160
```

```
220   IF S = 0 THEN 250 : FOR K = 1 TO S
230   FOR J = 52 TO 2 STEP −1
240   R = RND(J) + 1 : C = D(R) : D(R) = D(J) : D(J) = C : NEXT J,K
250   PRINT "CARD DECK ORDER" : C = 1
260   FOR J = 1 TO 52 : TAB C
290   V = D(J) MOD 13 : IF V>8 THEN 300 : PRINT V + 2 : GOTO 310
300   PRINT F$(V−8,V−8);
310   S = D(J)/13 + 1
320   PRINT S$(S,S);
330   C = C + 4 : IF C<37 THEN 340 : C = 1 : PRINT
340   NEXT J : PRINT
350   INPUT "ENTER 'Q' TO QUIT!",Q$ : IF Q$ = "Q" THEN 400
360   INPUT "ENTER 'N' FOR NEW DECK!",Q$ : IF Q$ = "N" THEN 140
370   GOTO 165
400   END
```

The following are the instructions in the RND program needed to shuffle a deck of cards.

1. A zero (0) shuffle—prints out the deck of cards in the following order of suits: spades, hearts, diamonds, and clubs.
2. A negative number input—gives a comic comment to the operator.
3. Over 8 shuffles—gives a probability comment, but will allow the operator to shuffle the deck over 8 times.

The variables used in the program are D = DECK OF CARDS, S$ = SUIT, F$ = FACE CARDS, and Q$ for "Q" (quit) or "T" (try again). Line 120 DIMensions D(DECK) to 52 cards, S$(SUIT) to 4 suits, F$(FACE CARDS) to 4, and Q$(1) for a "T" (try again) or "Q" for quit.

Line 140 is the beginning of a loop used to put the cards in the deck in memory. Line 150 D(J) = J − 1 is a method to overcome the deficiency of truncation. By subtracting 1 from J (J−1), the deck of cards is placed in memory from 0 (zero) to 51. When the card values (V) are operated on, 0 (zero) to 12 gives the cards of the spades suit (deuce through the ace). The statement in line 290, V = D(J) MOD 13, gives the value of the card. The statement of line 310, S = D(J)/13 + 1, gives the suit of the card. The spade suit equals $(0 - 12)/13 + 1 = 1$, the heart suit equals $(13 - 25)/13 + 1 = 2$, the diamond suit equals $(26 - 38)/13 + 1 = 3$, and the club suit equals $(39 - 51)/13 + 1 = 4$.

Line 160 starts the sequence with a fresh deck of cards and line 165 asks for the number of times the deck is to be shuffled.

If the line 170 statement of IF S > = 0 is true, the program defaults to line 180 for a sarcastic comment. If S > = 0 is false, the program branches to line 190 to check that the number of times the deck is shuffled is less than 8. If the shuffle is less than 8 times, the program branches to line 220. If the shuffle is zero times, the deck is printed out in its original order—spades: 2 to ace, hearts: 2 to ace, etc. If the shuffle is from 1 to 8 times, the statement of line 220, FOR K = 1 TO S, begins its execution. The inner loop of line 230, FOR J = 52 to 2 STEP −1, sets up the shuffle.

Line 240 statement R = RND(J) + 1 randomizes the cards. C=D(R) : D(R) = D(J) : D(J) = C causes the cards to be exchanged and the NEXT J,K completes the loop structures.

Line 250 prints out the heading, "CARD DECK ORDER," and sets the variable C = 1.

Line 260 is the beginning of the loop to output the cards. TAB C tabs to column 1.

The statement of line 290, V = D(J) MOD 13, sets up the value of the cards from 0 (zero) to 8 for the number cards. If the number card is greater than 8, the program branches to output the face cards of the suit. The comment, PRINT V + 2, adds 2 to each numbered suit card (remember, the cards were stored 0 to 51) so the deuce is printed out as a 2 (not a 0). The comment, GOTO 310, divides the suits into 13 cards and line 320 prints out the suit. Thus, the face cards, the number cards, and the suits have been printed out.

Line 330 statement, C = C + 4, causes 4 spaces between outputs, while the comment IF C<37 THEN 340 causes a printout until 37 columns have been filled. Finally, C = 1 sets the column back to 1 and the PRINT comment closes out the line.

The line 340 statement of NEXT J closes out the loop.

The rest of the program has been explained before even though it was in a different form. Probably the most used function in Integer BASIC is the RND function. Many games base their "opportunity for chance" programs on the RND function.

EXERCISES

1. Define ten new words from your computer dictionary.

2. Use the RND function to develop a game that is commonly referred to as CRAPS.

LESSON 17

Efficient Programming

After you have completed Lesson 17, you should be able to:

1. Program more efficiently.

EXAMPLE PROGRAMS

The first program is an example of an inefficient program. The program solves the problem and produces an output in the proper format. All in all, the program works fine for the hobbyist and there is absolutely nothing wrong with it. However, if the grade range from 0 to 100, by increments of 10, was developed, the program would be about 300% longer. For the sake of brevity, only the grades from 71 to 100 are legal input.

A = AVERAGE, C = COUNTING VARIABLE, D9 – D7 = GRADE RANGE
VARIABLES, T = TOTAL

```
110  REM*INEFFICIENT PROGRAM TO AVERAGE
120  REM*GRADES & OUTPUT RANGES
130  REM*GRADES BELOW 71 NOT ACCEPTED
140  C = 0 : D9 = 0 : D8 = 0 : D7 = 0 : T = 0
150  INPUT G
160  IF G>100 OR G<71 THEN 260
170  C = C + 1
180  T = T + G
190  IF G<91 THEN 210
200  D9 = D9 + 1 : GOTO 150
210  IF G<81 THEN 230
220  D8 = D8 + 1 : GOTO 150
230  IF G<71 THEN 250
240  D7 = D7 + 1 : GOTO 150
```

```
250   GOTO 150
260   A = T/C
270   PRINT "TOTAL # OF GRADES  = ";C
280   PRINT "AVERAGE OF GRADES  = ";A
290   PRINT "RANGE 91 TO 100    = ";D9
300   PRINT "RANGE 81 TO 90     = ";D8
310   PRINT "RANGE 71 TO 80     = ";D7
320   END
```

The preceding program is inefficient because it has four deficiencies: (1) the range variables (D9, etc.) are individually initialized to zero, (2) a separate decision statement is used to break out the grade ranges, (3) numerous GOTO statements are used (including a GOTO 250 statement when line 250 is a GOTO statement), and (4) separate PRINT statements are used to output the results.

Table 17-1 compares a list of the inefficient methods of Program 1 (to program the grade range problem) versus a list of the efficient methods used in Program 2.

Table 17-1. Comparison of Program Methods

INEFFICIENT	EFFICIENT

1. Variables are initialized singly.
    D9 = 0 : D8 = 0 : D7 = 0
	1. Variables are initialized using subscripts in a loop.
	    DIM N(9)
	    FOR D9 = 0 TO 9 : N(D9) = 0 :
	    NEXT D9

2. Decision statement is used to break out each grade range.
    IF G<91 THEN 210
    IF G<81 THEN 230
    IF G<71 THEN 250
	2. Formula is used to determine grade ranges.
	    N((G−1)/10) + N((G−1)/10) + 1

3. Numerous GOTO statements are used.
    GOTO 150
    GOTO 150
    GOTO 150
    A GOTO statement is used to move to a GOTO statement.
    230   IF G<71 THEN 250
    250   GOTO 150
	3. Only one GOTO statement is used.
	    220 GOTO 170

4. Separate PRINT statements are used to output grade ranges.
    PRINT "RANGE 91 TO 100"
    PRINT "RANGE 81 TO 90"
    PRINT "RANGE 71 TO 80"
	4. Loop and PRINT statements are used to output grade ranges.
	    FOR D9 = 9 TO 0 STEP −1
	    L = (D9 + 1) * 10
	    M = (D9 * 10) + 1
	    IF D9 = 0 THEN M = 0
	    PRINT M; "TO";L; " ";N(D9)
	    NEXT D9

Now, let us examine an efficient program.

L = MAXIMUM, M = MINIMUM, N = NUMBER OF GRADES

```
110  REM*EFFICIENT PROGRAM TO AVERAGE
120  REM*GRADES & OUTPUT RANGES
130  REM
140  DIM N(9), Q$(1)
150  FOR D9 = 0 TO 9 : N(D9) = 0 : NEXT D9
160  C = 0 : T = 0
170  INPUT G
180  IF G>100 OR G<0 THEN 230
190  C = C + 1
200  T = T + G
210  N((G−1)/10) = N((G−1)/10) + 1
220  GOTO 170
230  A = T/C
240  PRINT "TOTAL # OF GRADES = ";C
250  PRINT "AVERAGE OF GRADES = ";A
260  FOR D9 = 9 TO 0 STEP −1
270  L = (D9 + 1) * 10
280  M = (D9 * 10) + 1
290  IF D9 = 0 THEN M = 0
300  PRINT M; "TO";L; "        ";N(D9)
310  NEXT D9
320  END
```

The development of an efficient program begins with a problem statement and an output format. The most efficient way to initialize several variables using Integer BASIC is to use a subscripted variable in a loop.

```
DIM N(9)
FOR D9 = 0 TO 9 : N(D9) = 0 : NEXT D9
```

D9 (VARIABLE)	N(D9) (SUBSCRIPTED VARIABLE)
D9 = 0	0
D9 = 1	0
D9 = 2	0
D9 = 3	0
D9 = 4	0
D9 = 5	0
D9 = 6	0
D9 = 7	0
D9 = 8	0
D9 = 9	0

The formula for grade ranges is developed by logic using chart forms. In programming, anything that can be placed in a formula is more efficient than an individual decision statement. If one formula will not cover all possibilities, perhaps two or more formulae breakdowns will cover all possibilities. In this program, one formula is used to accommodate the grade input in relation to the grade output.

The first step is to develop a formula to determine the subscripted value of N that is consistent with the grade ranges of the distribution. The formula for the subscript is found by trial and error. What formula will give a changing subscript value that also relates to the minimum and maximum values of the grade ranges? Remember, Integer BASIC truncates. We know that the grades will range from 0 (zero) to 100, and the top range is from 91 to 100. Since $91 - 1$ divided by 10 truncates to 9, the bottom of the range is at the proper level. One hundred $(100) - 1$ divided by 10 truncates to 9, so the top of the range remains in the proper limit. The subscripted value (9) covers all grades from 91 to 100 so this trial gives a formula of $(G - 1)/10 =$ the subscripted value. The range is divided to give a reduced subscript value and, conversely, the subscript value is multiplied to give an increased range value. This is shown in Table 17-2.

Table 17-2. Grade Ranges

Grade Range	COMPUTATION	=	SUBSCRIPT VALUE
91	$91 - 1 = 90/10$		9
92	$92 - 1 = 91/10$		9
93	$93 - 1 = 92/10$		9
94	$94 - 1 = 93/10$		9
95	$95 - 1 = 94/10$		9
96	$96 - 1 = 95/10$		9
97	$97 - 1 = 96/10$		9
98	$98 - 1 = 97/10$		9
99	$99 - 1 = 98/10$		9
100	$100 - 1 = 99/10$		9

The subscript value (9) fits the range value (91 to 100). The grades from 91 to 100 must be divided to fit the grade range so $(G - 1)/10$ is the formula of the trial-and-error result. It is now nec-

Table 17-3. Determining Subscript Value

MIN	MAX	SUBSCRIPT	SUBSCRIPTED VARIABLE	FORMULA
91	100	9	N(9)	$(G-1)/10$
81	90	8	N(8)	$(G-1)/10$
71	80	7	N(7)	$(G-1)/10$
61	70	6	N(6)	$(G-1)/10$
51	60	5	N(5)	$(G-1)/10$
41	50	4	N(4)	$(G-1)/10$
31	40	3	N(3)	$(G-1)/10$
21	30	2	N(2)	$(G-1)/10$
11	20	1	N(1)	$(G-1)/10$
0	10	0	N(0)	$(G-1)/10$

N = VARIABLE   S = SUBSCRIPT

essary to determine if this formula fits all the grade inputs, in relation to the grade ranges. Table 17-3 shows the result.

From Table 17-3, it is seen that the formula for the subscript (S) necessary to separate the grade ranges is $(G-1)/10$. The variable N is incremented from 0 to 9 according to the grade ranges. The S (Subscript) Formula $= (G-1)/10$, and the subscript is to be incremented from 0 to 9 by 1. Thus, $N(S) = N(S) + 1$, and therefore, by substitution, the formula is developed to increment the subscripted variable in relation to the grade ranges. This is shown as follows:

$$S = (G-1)/10$$
$$N(S) = N(S) + 1$$
$$N((G-1)/10) = N((G-1)/10) + 1$$

What happens when a grade of zero is input? In this case, $(0 - 1) = -1$, which, when divided by 10, truncates to zero. This follows the formula because truncation eliminates the negative.

The line 220 statement, GOTO 170, is the only GOTO statement in the program. It sends the program back for another grade input.

To output the results, another formula must be determined. The grades have been categorized by ranges in increments of ten (91 to 100) and the number of grades ($N(D9)$) must be printed in each range. This is shown in Table 17-4.

Table 17-4. Determining Printout Formulae

VARIABLE (D9)	MIN	FORMULA	MAX	FORMULA
9	91	$(D9*10)+1$	100	$(D9+1)*10$
8	81	$(D9*10)+1$	90	$(D9+1)*10$
7	71	$(D9*10)+1$	80	$(D9+1)*10$
6	61	$(D9*10)+1$	70	$(D9+1)*10$
5	51	$(D9*10)+1$	60	$(D9+1)*10$
4	41	$(D9*10)+1$	50	$(D9+1)*10$
3	31	$(D9*10)+1$	40	$(D9+1)*10$
2	21	$(D9*10)+1$	30	$(D9+1)*10$
1	11	$(D9*10)+1$	20	$(D9+1)*10$
0	0	†	10	$(D9+1)*10$

† Formula does not work.

Again, the formula determination is made by trial and error. The formula for the minimum number in the range is $(D9*10)+1$. The formula for the maximum number in the range is $(D9+1)*10$. To simplify printing in line 300 of the program, a replacement statement is used for L (maximum). Since the minimum value does not follow a single formula, putting its value in a variable is most efficient. The formula does not work for the grade range 0 to 10 because there are eleven numbers in this range. To overcome this change, a decision statement is used. This is shown by line 290 statement of IF D9 = 0 THEN M = 0. The formula will only print out grades in the 1 to 10 range.

Now that all parts of the 0 to 100 range are covered, and all grades have been input, the line 220 statement of GOTO 170 causes the program to branch to the line 170 statement, INPUT G.

The line 180 statement is IF G>100 OR G<0 THEN 230. If a grade above 100 or a grade below 0 (zero) is input, the program will branch to line 230 to average the grades and begin the printout. Line 240 causes the total number of grades to be printed out, and line 250 causes the average of all the grades to be printed.

The grade ranges and the total number of grades in a specific range are printed out using a FOR loop. Line 260 statement of FOR D9 = 9 TO 0 STEP −1 is the beginning of the loop that prepares to output the ranges, beginning with the 91 to 100 range and decrementing by 10 for each range to the 0 to 10 range.

The L = (D9+1)*10 statement on line 270 sets the maximum for each range, while the line 280 statement of M = (D9*10)+1 sets the minimum for each range.

The line 290 statement of IF D9 = 0 THEN M = 0 is the decision statement that prepares the 0 to 10 range to output 11 numbers instead of 10, and line 300 causes a printout with PRINT M (minimum range); "TO";L(maximum range); "   ";N(D9) (number of grades in each range).

Finally, the line 310 statement, NEXT D9, is the end of the loop and line 320 ENDs the program. After looking at the work needed to develop an efficient program, maybe the inefficient program is the best after all. Seriously though, for maximum utilization of the system, the efficient program is superior in time, effort, and MONEY. This is a profit-oriented society, and money is what it's all about.

In relation to computer speed, there are two parameters—memory and compute time. Generally, the more memory used, the less the compute time will be and vice-versa (the less memory used the more the compute time will be). The speed relationship for the fastest to slowest parts of the system is: (1) compute, (2) memory, (3) input-output (I/O), (4) modem, and, finally, (5) printers and cassette devices. System efficiency demands a maximum utilization of the slowest peripherals. The fast units in the system can be programmed around the slow units.

There are some methods to make programs run faster. For example: (1) omit REMark statements or place them after the end of the program, (2) use one letter variables and reuse the same variables where possible, (3) use FOR NEXT loops instead of IF THEN loops, (4) place several statements on each line number and separate them by colons, and (5) calculate common subexpressions and place the value in a variable; i.e., $L = (D9+1)*10$.

While speed, efficiency, and formula programming are important in the business world, these factors are not that important to the hobbyist. If you have a program that works for you and it solves your problem, then that is why you bought the computer. Speed and efficiency aren't that important! Have fun and enjoy your hobby.

EXERCISES

1. Define ten new words from your computer dictionary.

2. Rewrite the efficient average program using different variables and construct the tables to develop the formulae used in the program.

Graphics

After completion of this lesson, you should be able to:

1. Use graphics to enhance data output.
2. Use two methods of scaling graphic output to utilize graphic functions.

VOCABULARY

COLOR—In the standard resolution color (GR) mode, the COLOR = 12 command sets the tv screen color to the value in the expression (for a range of colors from 0 to 15).

GR—sets mixed standard resolution color graphics mode. Initializes COLOR = 0 (Black) for top 40 × 40 portion of screen, and sets the scrolling window to lines 21 to 24 (× 40 characters) for four lines of TEXT at the bottom of the screen.

HLIN—In the standard resolution color graphics mode, the HLIN 0,39 AT 20 command draws a horizontal line of a predefined color (starting at the horizontal position defined by the expression and ending at the position defined by the expression) and AT a vertical position that is defined by the expression (in the range of 0 to 39).

Pause loop—a method of controlled interruption of a program.

PEEK—a command to examine a memory location.

POKE—a command to put something into a memory location.

PLOT—In standard resolution color graphics, the PLOT 15,25 command plots a small square of a predefined color (set by COLOR =) at a horizontal location specified by the expression (in a range 0 to 39) and at a vertical location specified by expression (in the range of 0 to 39). Note: PLOT 0,0 is the square in the upper left-most position and PLOT 39,39 is the pixel in the lower right corner.

Reserved words—words reserved by the language (Integer BASIC) for commands, operators, functions, and statements.

Scaling—the process of altering a set of quantities by a fixed quantity so as to bring the values within the limits capable of being handled by the equipment or routines that are being used.

TEXT—sets the TEXT mode. Screen is formatted to display alphanumeric characters on 24 lines of 40 characters each. TEXT resets scrolling window to the maximum.

VLIN—Similar to the HLIN command except that it draws a vertical line starting at the position specified. For the command, VLIN 0,39 AT 15, it starts at 0 and ends at 39, at the horizontal position of 15.

EXAMPLE PROGRAM

This lesson is a graphic presentation of the GRADE RANGE program given in Lesson 17. The GRaphics program is a continuation of the GRADE RANGE program. To bring the two programs into one program, place the GRADE RANGE program in memory and type in 320 to add the first line of the GRaphics program (also change line 140 DIM N(D9), Q$(1). The single GRaphics program outputs the grade ranges in both numerics and graphics.

The Apple II microcomputer is designed to provide a color graphics output of two types: (1) low-resolution or color graphics, and (2) high-resolution graphics. Only low-resolution graphics will be discussed in this book.

A list of the variables used in the program and their explanation follows.

D = number of grades in the grade range that has the least number of grades (Example: if 81 to 90 has only 2 grades and 2 is the smallest number of grades that are in any range, then, D = 2 (minimum)).

S = number of grades in the grade range that has the greatest number of grades (Example: if 71 to 80 has 30 grades and 30 is the maximum number of grades that are in any grade, then, the range S = 30 (maximum)).

S − D = difference between maximum number of grades and minimum number of grades (max − min).

J = number of pluses (+) to be printed for a specific grade range.

L = maximum of grade range (same as S).

M = minimum of grade range (same as D).

```
110   REM*EFFICIENT PROGRAM TO AVERAGE
120   REM*GRADES & OUTPUT RANGES
130   REM
140   DIM N(9), Q$(1)
150   FOR D9 = 0 TO 9 : N(D9) = 0 : NEXT D9
160   C = 0 : T = 0
170   INPUT G
180   IF G>100 OR G<0 THEN 230
190   C = C + 1
200   T = T + G
210   N((G − 1)/10) = N((G − 1)/10) + 1
220   GOTO 170
230   A = T/C
240   PRINT "TOTAL # OF GRADES = ";C
250   PRINT AVERAGE OF GRADES = ";A
260   FOR D9 = 9 TO 0 STEP −1
270   L = (D9 + 1) * 10
280   M = (D9 * 10) + 1
290   IF D9 = 0 THEN M = 0
300   PRINT M; "TO";L;"      ";N(D9)
310   NEXT D9
320   S = N(0) : D = N(0)
330   FOR D9 = 1 TO 9 : IF N(D9)>S THEN S = N(D9) : IF N(D9)<D
      THEN D = N(D9) : NEXT D9
335   PRINT "ENTER LINE NUMBER FOR UNUSUAL BRANCH" : PRINT "'170'
      TO INPUT" : PRINT "'240' FOR STATISTICS"
337   PRINT "'000' TO CONTINUE" : INPUT "'−01' TO END",P : IF P<0
      THEN 998 : IF P = 0 THEN 340 : GOTO P
340   PRINT "ENTER 'D' TO END AFTER COLOR GRAPH!" : TAB 7 : INPUT "'S'
      TO SKIP COLOR GRAPH!",Q$ : IF Q$ = "S" THEN 470
350   CALL −936 : GR : COLOR = 15
360   VLIN 0,39 AT 0
370   HLIN 0,39 AT 39
380   VTAB 21 : PRINT "   0  11  21  31  41  51  61  71  81  91  100"
390   VTAB 22 : PRINT "  TO  TO  TO  TO  TO  TO  TO  TO  TO  TO"
400   VTAB 23 : PRINT "  10  20  30  40  50  60  70  80  90  100";
410   FOR D9 = 0 TO 9
420   COLOR = D9 + 3
430   VLIN 39 − N(D9)*39/S,39 AT D9*4 + 2
440   NEXT D9
450   IF Q$ = "D" THEN 998
460   FOR D9 = 1 TO 15000 : NEXT D9
470   TEXT : CALL −936 : IF S = D THEN D = S − 1
480   TAB 4 : PRINT "SCALED DISTRIBUTION GRAPH"
490   FOR D9 = 1 TO 21
500   IF D9/2*2 = D9 THEN 540
510   PRINT "     *"; : IF D9<21 THEN 630
520   TAB 11 : PRINT D; : TAB 39 −(S>9) − (S>99) : PRINT S
530   GOTO 630
540   M = ((D9/2−1)*10)+1 : IF D9 = 2 THEN M = 0
560   L = D9*5
570   PRINT M; : TAB 4 : PRINT "TO"; : TAB 7 : PRINT L; : TAB 10 :
      PRINT "*";
580   J = (N(D9/2−1)−D)*28/(S−D)
590   FOR K = 0 TO J
```

```
600   PRINT "+";
610   NEXT K
630   PRINT : NEXT D9
998   VTAB 23 : END
999   TEXT : CALL −936 : END
```

Line 320 statement of S = N(0) : D = N(0) sets the maximum number of grades (S = N(0)) and, also, sets the minimum number of grades (D = N(0)) to zero. Line 330 searches the other grade ranges (N(1 to 9)) to select both the grade range with the maximum number of grades and the grade range with the minimum number of grades.

Lines 335, 337, and 340 enable the operator to print out different sections of the program and to add grades if desired. The following notations are used:

> 170   to input more grades.
> 240   to view grades and grade ranges.
> 000   to continue the program.
> D   to end the program after the color graph display.
> S   to skip the color graph.
> −01   to end the program.

Line 350 statement, CALL −936, clears the screen, while the line 350 statement of GR places the computer in the low-resolution (color) graphics mode and draws an all-black plotting surface. The line 350 statement of COLOR = 15 sets the drawing color to white. Color is a reserved word which reserves the color to draw on the black plotting surface. An Apple II microcomputer used with a color-tv screen has these colors available.

0	BLACK	8	BROWN
1	MAGENTA	9	ORANGE
2	DARK BLUE	10	GREY
3	PURPLE	11	PINK
4	DARK GREEN	12	GREEN
5	GREY	13	YELLOW
6	MEDIUM BLUE	14	AQUA
7	LIGHT BLUE	15	WHITE

Line 360 has the statement VLIN 0,39 AT 39. The VDM screen is set as in the lower right-hand quadrant of an X,Y axis but the value of Y is positive instead of negative, as shown in Fig. 18-1. The screen coordinates are set in the manner shown in Fig. 18-2. The notation (X,Y) is a standard math representation of two dimensions on a graph. The Apple II microcomputer recognizes X as the first dimension, and Y as the second dimension in the X,Y pair, i.e., horizontal,

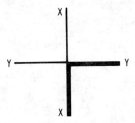

**Fig. 18-1. The X,Y axis on a
VDM screen.**

then vertical. The statement on line 370, HLIN 0,39 AT 39, draws the horizontal line at the bottom of the graph.

Lines 380, 390, and 400 tab vertically to the proper line and print out the grade ranges below the chart. The graphics mode splits the screen between graphics and text, so four lines of text can be placed at the bottom of the screen and four lines of text printed at the top of the screen.

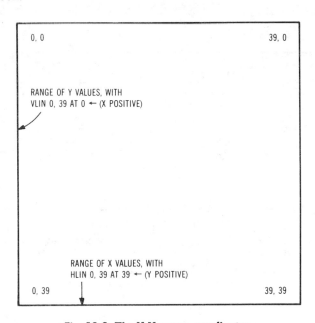

Fig. 18-2. The X,Y screen coordinates.

There are two ways to use full screen for low-resolution graphics.

1. GR : POKE −16302,0 (or, if in GR, use POKE −16302,0)
2. POKE −16304,0

To go from full screen graphics to TEXT, use:

1. TEXT
2. POKE −16303,0

To go from full screen to split screen, use:

1. POKE −16301,0

Lines 410 through 440 draw the 10 bars for each of the grade ranges. Line 410 is the beginning of the FOR loop necessary to access N(0) to N(9). Line 420 sets the color value to a different value for each range, as shown by the listing given in Table 18-1.

Line 430 statement is VLIN 39−N(D9)∗39/S,39 AT D9∗4 + 2. This line is used to cause a printout of the number of grades in each grade range. To digress, VLIN 0,39 AT 0 plots a vertical line from space zero (0) to space 39 in column 0 (zero). The variable S represents the maximum number of grades of all grade ranges.

The statement N(D9)∗39/S is a simple method used to determine the length of the bar graph for the 10 grade ranges from space 0 to 39. The line 0,39 reaches from the top of the screen to the bot-

Table 18-1. Color and Vertical Line Positions

D9	D9 + 3 (COLOR = D9 + 3)		D9∗4 + 2 (VERTICAL LINE POSITION)
0	3	purple	2
1	4	dark green	6
2	5	grey	10
3	6	medium blue	14
4	7	light blue	18
5	8	brown	22
6	9	orange	26
7	10	grey	30
8	11	pink	34
9	12	green	38

tom of the screen at the level of the horizontal white line axis. When N(D9) = S (i.e., N(D9) is maximum), N(D9)∗39/S is the same as N(D9)∗39/N(D9), and this truncates to 39. Thirty-nine (39) in the vertical direction is an area at the bottom line of the screen. When N(D9) is maximum, it will equal 39. From the formula, 39 − 39 = 0. The range for VLIN is 0 to 39; this is shown in Table 18-2.

This method of scaling expands small values to fill the screen and shrinks large values so the maximum range always prints a bar graph from zero to thirty-nine (0,39). If the scale was one to one (5 grades are represented by 5 squares), the distribution count would graph only if there were less than 39 grades in one grade range. If there were over 39 grades in one grade range, the program would bomb out. There are two deficiencies to this graphics mode:

Table 18-2. Table To Determine X,Y Coordinates and Row

D9	N(D9)	N(D9)=S (LENGTH OF LINE)	Y RANGES	D9*4+2 (X COLUMN WHERE LINE IS PRINTED)
9	3	39−3*39/31	36,39	38
8	9	39−9*39/31	28,39	34
7	31†	39−31*39/31	0,39	30
6	18	39−18*39/31	19,39	26
5	6	39−6*39/31	32,39	22
4	6	39−6*39/31	32,39	18
3	2	39−2*39/31	37,39	14
2	1	39−1*39/31	38,39	10
1	3	39−3*39/31	36,39	6
0	6	39−6*39/31	32,39	2

† N(D9) = S : S = 31 causes the maximum number to be utilized in the 71 to 80 grade range, so the bar graph line will extend from space 0 to 9.

(1) the vertical axis cannot be labeled, and (2) the bar graphs are not very accurate. The vertical axis can be labeled using TEXT graphics. High-resolution graphics can give a greater accuracy but, then, the vertical axis cannot be labeled.

The line 440 statement, NEXT D9, completes the loop, Then, the line 450 statement of IF Q$ = "D" THEN 998 skips the TEXT graph if "D" is input, while the statement in line 460, FOR D9 = 1 TO 15000 : NEXT D9, is a pause loop that is executed 15,000 times in order to let the operator view the bar graph distribution before the program goes to the TEXT graph of grade distribution.

Pause loops (technically, it may not be a loop) are used to control a program so that the user can view and study the output before the program continues. Pause loops may be placed anywhere in the program where a delay is desired. Four types of pause loops will be presented.

1. Loop delays program and, then, lets program continue without any operator action. Loop may be any length.

```
100   FOR D9 = 1 TO 15000 : NEXT D9
```

2. Loop pauses after a specific number of executions and then continues without operator action. In the following example, the pause is after every 20 executions. The number of executions can be changed to fit the program.

```
100   FOR I = 1 TO 100
110   Other functions may
120   be included in relation to the program
130   FOR I # I/20*20
140   FOR J = 1 TO 10000 : NEXT J
150   NEXT I
```

129

3. A loop that delays operation until the operator presses RE-TURN.

```
450   INPUT "PRESS 'RETURN' TO CONTINUE",A$   (A$ does not need to be
                                               dimensioned)
```

4. A loop that delays operation until the operator presses any key on the keyboard (except RESET).

```
10   IF PEEK (−16384)>127 THEN 20 : POKE −16368,0 : GOTO 10
20   POKE −16368,0
```

The line 470 statement is TEXT : CALL −936 : IF S = D THEN S = D − 1. TEXT puts the screen back into full text mode. CALL −936 clears the screen. The statement of IF S = D THEN S = D −1 is a safety feature. D is the minimum value of the number of grades from all grade ranges. If the minimum number is the same as the maximum number (S), the scaling mechanism will not function correctly. The TEXT graph is different from the GR graph. The GR graph scaled all bar ranges from the value zero (0). The TEXT graph ignores any range below the minimum number of grades. If the minimum number of grades in the TEXT graph is 5, the graph will start at 5 and plot to the maximum number of grades. However, if the minimum number of grades is zero (0), 0 will be the minimum location on the TEXT graph. No useful graphic information is gained by printing out below the minimum.

Line 480 TABs the microcomputer screen to column 4 and prints out the "SCALED DISTRIBUTION GRAPH" heading.

Line 490 statement is the beginning of a series of nested loops used to print the 21 lines of output that will comprise the graph.

Line 500 statement of IF D9/2*2 = D9 THEN 540 is a decision statement used to draw a grade range (lines 540 to 610) when D9 is an even number. When D9 is an odd number, an asterisk is printed in the vertical axis of the graph. When D9 is 1, the 1 divided by 2 (or 1/2) is zero and zero times 2 is zero (D9 = 1/2*2 = 0). Truncation can be used to split the number into odd-even factors, or any combination, based on 3, 4, etc. (IF D9 MOD 2 = 0 THEN 540 does the same thing. If D9 = 2, then 2/2*2 = 2). If D9 is odd, line 500 defaults to line 510 and prints out an asterisk in column 10; it leaves the line "open" (the next print will continue after the asterisk). If D9 is 21, line 510 defaults to line 520 so as to tab to column 11 and print a D (the minimum number of grades) and an S (the maximum number of grades).

Line 520 contains the statement TAB 39−(S>9)−(S>99). If S is 9 or less, the tab value ends at 39. If S is 10 to 99, the tab value is 38. This is necessary so that a 2-digit number for S will end in the 39 column. For example:

	COLUMN		
S =	37	38	39
9			9
12		1	2
409	4	0	9

The term S>9 is logical. If S is greater than 9, then S>9 is equal to 1 (logical true) and 1 is subtracted from 39. If S is greater than 99, S>99 is equal to 1 (logical true) and a 1 is subtracted from 39. The quotes surrounding (S>9) and (S>99) are essential. Try the problem without them and see what happens.

The statement contained in line 530 causes the loop execution to line 630 where all branches terminate.

The line 540 entry of M = ((D9/2−1)∗10)+1 : IF D9 = 2 THEN M = 0 is a program statement where even values of D9 are processed. M is the coding for the minimum value of the grade ranges and L is the code for the maximum value of the grade ranges.

Line 490 statement of D9 = 1 TO 21 is used as the base to print out the bars on the TEXT graph. The bars are printed on even numbered values of D9. The problem is to tie the length of the bar (number of grades per grade range) to the grade ranges themselves. This is illustrated in Table 18-3. To correct the range from zero (0) to 10 use IF D9 = 2 THEN M = 0.

Table 18-3. Relating Line Numbers to Grade Ranges

D9 (even values 2–20)	M = ((D9/2−1)∗10)+1	L = D9∗5
2	1 †	10
4	11	20
6	21	30
8	31	40
10	41	50
12	51	60
14	61	70
16	71	80
18	81	90
20	91	100

† Does not follow formula.

The line 570 statement causes the range labeling to the left of the vertical axis (Y axis) to be printed. It also tabs to align the "TOs". The semicolon after the asterisk tells the machine to continue printing on the same line.

The statement J = (N(D9/2−1)−D)∗28/(S−D) on line 580 calculates the number of pluses (+) to be printed out. The pluses represent the number of grades in each grade range. The quantity $(S-D)$ is the difference between the maximum number of grades and the minimum number of grades. The term $(D9/2-1)$ adjusts D9 for the range to go from 2 to 20 and from 0 to 9, so 0 to 9 can be used as the subscript.

When $N(D9/2-1)$ in the statement is the minimum number of grades, and D (minimum number of grades) is subtracted, the result is zero. Zero carried through the expression gives a result of zero. When the N value is equal to the maximum number of grades, the formula can be represented as $(S-D)*28/(S-D)$ or 28. The MIN-MAX range of values is from 0 to 28.

Lines 590 through 610 contain a loop that will print out the bars on the bar graph. If J is 0, the loop is executed one time to print 1 plus $(+)$ to show the minimum number of grades in the proper grade range. If the minimum number of grades is 5, only one "plus" will be printed. No useful information is derived from printing the minimum as more than one plus. The maximum number of grades in a specific grade range is printed out as 29 pluses. The FOR $K = 0$ TO J loop statement prints out one time for the zero execution; this is the same as $J + 1$.

The line 630 statement of PRINT : NEXT D9 is the joining place for all three branches of the loop, and it is also the end of the loop. The PRINT statement closes out the line.

The line 998 VTAB 23 : END statement leaves the cursor at line 23 and ENDs the program.

Line 999 can never be accessed directly by the program. The operator must access line 999 by using a GOTO 999 statement to restore the TEXT mode to the screen.

The RUN mode allows the user to enter the number of grades to be input. After data has been entered, the following statements are printed on the screen:

```
ENTER '170' FOR INPUT
      '240' FOR STATISTICS
      '000' TO CONTINUE
            ('D' TO END AFTER COLOR GRAPH!
            'S' TO SKIP COLOR GRAPH)
      '-01' TO END
```

Typing '000' to continue brings us the statement of 'D' TO END AFTER COLOR GRAPH or 'S' TO SKIP COLOR GRAPH. When 'D' is entered, the screen is left in the graphics mode. To change this mode, type in TEXT. What caused this? The machine is sending graphics to the screen in TEXT format. To redisplay the graph, type in GOTO 350. This will cause the program to restart at line 350. Type GOTO 999 to restore TEXT mode and to clear the screen.

Type in GOTO 340. The program asks for input. Type in 'S'. The graphics are bypassed and the TEXT plot is drawn. The TEXT plot is scaled from minimum to maximum. If the minimum and the maximum were the same values, the program would "bomb" because *"thou shalt not divide by zero."* The third statement in line 470 overcomes this problem, so a zero will not be produced. By this logic, when $S/(S-D)$, the substitution is the same as $S-(S-1) = S-S$ $+1 = 1$. The TEXT scaling is different from the GR plot because the GR plot ranges from zero to maximum, while the TEXT plot ranges from minimum to maximum. To change the GR plot from minimum to maximum, just change line 430 to:

```
430  VLIN 39−(N(D9)−D)∗39/(S−D), 39 AT D9∗4+2
```
(If S−D equals zero (0), you will get a division by zero error.)

To prevent a division by zero error, take the IF statement in line 470 (IF S = D THEN D = S − 1), and create a new line number 333 (333 IF S = D THEN D = S −1), and delete the IF statement in line 470. This will prevent the program from having a division by zero error. This technique is necessary to subtract off the minimum number of grades and divide by the difference (S−D).

Again, type in GOTO 340. The program asks for input. Just press RETURN. The GRaphics plot is displayed. The program then defaults to line 460, the delay loop. The delay loop produces a certain amount of time to allow the graphics plot to be viewed before the TEXT plot is output.

The GOTO 240 statement reproduces the statistics of the program, and the GOTO 170 statement allows more grades to be input and will count them with the grades previously input. This is convenient if the input is ended prematurely.

Why was GOTO 340 typed in and not RUN 340? If RUN 340 is input, a >32767 ERR is produced. All values are zeroed, and dividing by zero is illegal.

The tv screen on the set used by the author bleeds the white on the bottom (horizontal) axis over the base of the bar. To correct this condition, the white square to the left of the bar can be blacked out. Rather than drawing a vertical or horizontal line of one square, a PLOT function is used. COLOR is set to zero (COLOR = 0 is black). The color bars at X are equal to D9∗4+2. The value of X to the left of each bar is D9∗4+1. The value of Y at the base is 39, and does not change. Where should the changes be made? First, they should be made in the same loop that draws each of the ten bars and, secondly, the change can be made before or after the bar is plotted. Since line 440 is short, the change is added to line 440 as follows:

```
440  COLOR = 0 : PLOT D9∗4+1,39 : NEXT D9
```

The PLOT could have been placed before the bar drawing.

```
410   FOR D9 = 0 TO 9 : COLOR = 0 : PLOT D9*4+1,39
420   COLOR = 0 : PLOT D9*4+1,39 : COLOR = D9+3
```

Table 18-4. Synopsis of Limits

CONDITION	FUNCTION	VERTICAL RANGE	HORIZONTAL RANGE
Text	VTAB	1 to 24	—
Text	TAB	—	1 to 40
Split Screen	PLOT	0 to 39	0 to 39
Split Screen	VTAB	—	21 to 24 †
Full Screen	PLOT	0 to 47	0 to 39
	COLOR	0 to 15	0 to 15

† Lines 21 to 24 with 40 characters each.

A synopsis of the limits of the tv-monitor line lengths is given in Table 18-4. Note that lines 21 through 24 will each accommodate 40 characters to the line.

EXERCISES

1. Define ten new words from your computer dictionary.

2. Modify the delay loop so that it delays twice as long as in the GRaphics program.

3. Rewrite the GRaphics program using all new variables.

LESSON 19

Menu and Flag

You should be able, after completion of this lesson, to:

1. Program using a menu selection.
2. Use a flag (F) variable to aid in data information.

VOCABULARY

Flag—an additional piece of information added to a data item itself, e.g., an error flag will indicate that the data item has given rise to an error condition. The term is also used to refer to end of field and end of data markers.

Menu—a method of using a terminal to display a list of optional facilities which can be chosen by the user in order to carry out different functions in a system.

EXAMPLE PROGRAM

This lesson contains a self-explanatory program used to demonstrate menu and flag conditions. By typing in the numbers of the related headings shown in the menu, the program explains itself. The numbers should be followed in a sequential order from 1 to 8. The program should be studied to understand how to program using a menu. Menu selection is a common method to use when the operator has little knowledge of computers. Just a few suggestions about the program.

1. Remember when you edit program statements going from the end of one line to the beginning of the next line to use the ES-

CAPE key, then the A key. Place the cursor immediately after the last character on the line and, then, use the ESCAPE-then-A keying method to place the cursor over the first character on the next line. If you use the shift-right arrow, you will change the spacing between the lines.

2. The program type used in this book is for easy reading and it will not type exactly the same way into the computer. For example, the word "TO." If "T" ends on the first line of the program statement and "O" is the first character on the second line of the program statement, it is typed in the book as "TO" on one line.

3. Line 590 may look unusual (FOR S = 1 TO 8 : PRINT "   ";S, S*100 + 160 : NEXT S). Using a semicolon delimiter (;) will cause a horizontal printout and it squeezes the space out of the print, while a comma delimiter (,) prints out in the next available field.

S	S*100 + 160
1	260
2	360
3	460
4	560
5	660
6	760
7	860
8	960

4. There is no DIMension statement for Q$ because RETURN represents zero (0) memory locations. Any string that requires reserved memory requires a DIMension statement.

Type the following self-explanatory program into your microcomputer.

```
100  REM*PROGRAM TO EXPLAIN AND
110  REM*DEMONSTRATE MENU
120  REM* AND FLAG
130  F = 0
140  CALL -936
150  TAB 8 : PRINT "MENU EXPLANATION PROGRAM" : PRINT : PRINT
160  TAB 5 : PRINT "1. PRINT EXPLANATION"
170  TAB 5 : PRINT "2. LIST MENU"
180  TAB 5 : PRINT "3. LIST SAFETY CHECK"
190  TAB 5 : PRINT "4. LIST CALCULATION GOTO METHOD"
200  TAB 5 : PRINT "5. LIST IF GOTO METHOD #1" : TAB 5 :
     PRINT "6. LIST IF GOTO METHOD #2"
210  TAB 5 : PRINT "7. EXPLAIN F AS FLAG" : TAB 5 : PRINT "8. END"
220  PRINT : IF F THEN PRINT "ERROR CHECKING IS TURNED OFF" : TAB 10 :
     INPUT "SELECTION PLEASE",S : IF F THEN 240
```

```
230   IF S>0 AND S<9 THEN 240 : PRINT "***YOUR SELECTION IS INVALID" :
      PRINT "***PLEASE TRY AGAIN!" : GOTO 220
240   CALL -936
250   GOTO S*100 + 160
260   PRINT "WHEN A PROGRAM HAS SEVERAL CHOICES TO" : PRINT
270   PRINT "OFFER, A MENU SHOULD BE USED TO SHOW" : PRINT
280   PRINT "ALL OF THEM TO THE OPERATOR. THIS AL-" : PRINT
290   PRINT "LOWS THE GREATEST AMOUNT OF FLEXIBILI-" : PRINT
300   PRINT "TY OF USE" : PRINT
310   PRINT "(ALL THIS DOES IS PRINT A NUMBER" : PRINT
320   PRINT "BESIDE AN OPTION, THEN ASKS FOR AN "IN-" : PRINT
330   PRINT "PUT OF ONE OF THE NUMBERS." : PRINT
340   PRINT "TO SEE THE LISTING SELECT #2 NEXT.)" : PRINT
350   INPUT "PRESS 'RETURN' WHEN READY!",Q$ : GOTO 130
360   LIST 150, 220
370   PRINT : PRINT "THE MACHINE DOESN'T CARE WHICH NUMBER."
380   PRINT "IS BESIDE WHICH OPTION. THIS IS FOR"
390   PRINT "THE PROGRAMMER TO KEEP STRAIGHT."
400   PRINT "THE NUMBERS DON'T HAVE TO BE IN ORDER."
450   GOTO 350
460   LIST 230
470   PRINT : PRINT "FOR CARELESS PEOPLE OR SOMEONE WHO" : PRINT
480   PRINT "WANTS TO SEE IF THE PROGRAM CAN BE" : PRINT
490   PRINT "FOULED UP, IT IS BEST TO INSURE THAT" : PRINT
500   PRINT "THE RESPONSE IS 'LEGAL'" : PRINT
510   PRINT "THIS 'IF' PRINTED AN ERROR MESSAGE" : PRINT
520   PRINT "BUT DOING WITHOUT THIS IS SIMPLER" : PRINT
530   PRINT "(AS SHOWN BY THE EXAMPLE BELOW)." : PRINT
540   PRINT "230 IF S<1 OR S>8 THEN 130" : PRINT
550   GOTO 350
560   LIST 250
570   PRINT : PRINT "THIS IS THE CALCULATION METHOD" : PRINT
580   PRINT "VALUE OF S -- BRANCHES TO LINE"
590   FOR S = 1 TO 8 : PRINT "    " ; S, S*100 + 160 : NEXT S
600   PRINT : PRINT "IF NO ERROR CHECKING IS DONE, AN"
610   PRINT "ILLEGAL VALUE WILL BRANCH STRANGELY."
620   PRINT "S = 0 WILL GO TO 160 : S<0 OR S>8 WILL"
630   PRINT "CAUSE A BAD BRANCH ERR (YOU TOLD THE"
640   PRINT "MACHINE TO GO TO A NONEXISTENT LINE.)"
650   PRINT : PRINT "ENTER 1 TO TURN OFF ERROR CHECKING AND" : PRINT
      "TRY AN ILLEGAL VALUE" :  INPUT "OTHERWISE ENTER 0",F : GOTO 140
660   PRINT "WHEN THE CALCULATION METHOD CAN'T BE" : PRINT
670   PRINT "USED THE IF METHOD MUST BE APPLIED." : PRINT
680   PRINT "THIS VERSION TESTS FOR S EQUAL TO THE" : PRINT
690   PRINT "SPECIFIC VALUE. ERROR CHECKING DOES" : PRINT
700   PRINT "NOT NEED TO BE DONE FOR THIS TYPE." : PRINT
710   PRINT "240 IF S = 1 THEN 260" : PRINT "241 IF S = 2 THEN 360"
720   PRINT "242 IF S = 3 THEN 460" : PRINT "243 IF S = 4 THEN 560"
730   PRINT "244 IF S = 5 THEN 660" : PRINT "245 IF S = 6 THEN 760"
740   PRINT "246 IF S = 7 THEN 860" : PRINT "247 IF S = 8 THEN 960"
750   PRINT "248 GOTO 130 : PRINT : GOTO 350
760   PRINT "THIS IS A 2ND TYPE OF IF METHOD" : PRINT
770   PRINT "THIS IS A BIT TRICKIER BUT IS USEFUL" : PRINT
780   PRINT "WHEN YOU INTEND TO PUT THE BODY OF" : PRINT
790   PRINT "STATEMENTS DIRECTLY AFTER THE IF." : PRINT
```

```
800   PRINT "250 IF S # 1 THEN 360" : PRINT "360 IF S # 2 THEN 460"
810   PRINT "460 IF S # 3 THEN 560" : PRINT "560 IF S # 4 THEN 660" :
      PRINT "660 IF S # 5 THEN 760"
820   PRINT "760 IF S # 6 THEN 860" : PRINT "860 IF S # 7 THEN 960" :
      PRINT
830   PRINT "OF COURSE YOU WOULD HAVE THE BODY OF" : PRINT
      "STATEMENTS BETWEEN EACH IF."
840   PRINT "ERROR CHECKING HAS TO BE DONE FOR" : PRINT "THIS METHOD
      ELSE AN ERRONEOUS VALUE" : PRINT "WILL GO TO THE LAST
      POSSIBILITY."
850   PRINT "** FOR S = 3 THE IFS ARE TRUE UNTIL 460**" : GOTO 350
860   LIST 130 : LIST 220 : PRINT : PRINT "F IS A FLAG. IT SIGNIFIES A
      CONDITION." : PRINT : PRINT "THAT HAS OCCURRED OR THE USER
      WANTS."
870   PRINT : PRINT "LINE 130 INITIALLY SETS F'S VALUE" : PRINT : PRINT
      "TO SIGNIFY NO ACTION IS TO BE TAKEN."
880   PRINT : PRINT "IN LINE 220, IF F IS NONZERO THE MES-" : PRINT : PRINT
      "SAGE IS PRINTED AND THE IF IS TRUE."
890   PRINT : INPUT "PRESS 'RETURN' TO SEE THE NEXT PAGE",Q$ : CALL −936
900   LIST 650 : PRINT : PRINT "THIS STATEMENT IS THE PLACE WHERE" :
      PRINT : PRINT "F IS ALTERED BY THE USER." : PRINT
910   PRINT "THIS TOOK PLACE IN #4 TO SHOW WHAT" : PRINT : PRINT
      "HAPPENS WITH NO ERROR CHECKING." : PRINT
920   PRINT "'IF F THEN' IS FALSE ONLY IF F IS" : PRINT : PRINT "ZERO.
      ALL SECTIONS GOTO 130 TO RESET" : PRINT
930   PRINT "F TO 0 BUT LINE 650 (END OF #4 GOES" : PRINT : PRINT
      "TO 140 SO THIS DOESN'T HAPPEN.)" : PRINT
950   GOTO 350
960   TAB 15 : PRINT "THAT'S ALL!" : END
```

In the string program (Lesson 15), you were shown a subroutine that printed the error messages. That was one of the uses of a subroutine. It helped to compartmentalize the program so it could be written one part at a time. This purpose is somewhat defeated by the fact that you can GOSUB or GOTO at any line, whether it is a subroutine or not (larger machines handle this situation differently).

Another reason to use subroutines is to be able to use the same lines over and over again in different places. This saves programmer time and memory but increases compute time slightly. As a simple example, examine what line 350 (INPUT "PRESS 'RETURN' WHEN READY!",Q$: GOTO 130) does. All but sections 4 and 8 of the menu use line 350. The sections that do use it then GOTO 130.

If you want to execute line 350 and, then, continue on with different paths for all the sections, it is easy to convert line 350 to a small subroutine. To do this, the line should be:

```
350   INPUT "PRESS 'RETURN' WHEN READY.",Q$ : RETURN
```

The GOTO 130 has to be dropped.

To use this one line subroutine, each section of the menu would have to be changed to access it in the proper manner.

```
345   GOSUB 350 : GOTO 130
450   GOSUB 350 : GOTO 130
550   GOSUB 350 : GOTO 130
750   GOSUB 350 : GOTO 130
850   GOSUB 350 : GOTO 130
950   GOSUB 350 : GOTO 130
```

Now, there is a subroutine that can be used from six different places. This is a simple example, but it shows what can be done. In section No. 7, INPUT Q$ can be used to stop the printout before page No. 2. If line 890 is modified, it can shorten the program.

```
890   PRINT "NEXT PAGE"; : GOSUB 350 : CALL −936
```

These are examples of how a subroutine can be used to replace program statements.

EXERCISES

1. Define ten new words from your computer dictionary.

2. There are three types of depreciation—straight-line depreciation, sum of the year's digits depreciation, and double-declining balance depreciation. Using these three types of depreciation as a menu selection, write a program to compute the three types of depreciation.

LESSON 20

Games

After completing this lesson, you should be able to:

1. Program simple games.

EXAMPLE PROGRAMS

Two programs are presented in this lesson. CRAPS and FIVE CARD STUD are simple programs that are used to introduce you to this aspect of programming. The computer can store information, make decisions, and generate random numbers. This makes it an ideal tool for games.

Craps

The game of CRAPS is based on the RND function which permits the operator to roll the dice. If a 7 or 11 is rolled on the first throw, the win is a natural. If a number below 4 or a number over 11 is rolled on the first throw, the loss is a craps. If a 7 is rolled after a point has been assigned, it is also a loss. A point is a number that does not win or lose on the first roll. If a point of 8 is rolled, then 8 must be rolled again before a 7 is rolled.

To end the game, input "N". When "N" is input, the program prints out the wins, losses, and the total number of plays. The following list shows the playing codes.

    A = RND roll of 1 die.
    B = RND roll of 1 die.
    F = Flag

L1 = Number of losses.
 P = Point
 W = Number of wins
 X = Number produced by the roll of both dice.

```
5     REM* CRAPS
10    DIM L(6), Q$(1)
20    FOR I = 1 TO 6
30    L(I) = I
40    NEXT I
50    W = 0 : L1 = 0
60    F = 0 : P = 0
70    A = RND(6) + 1
80    B = RND(6) + 1
90    X = L(A) + L(B)
100   PRINT "ROLL OF DICE = ";X
110   IF F = 1 THEN 300
120   IF X = 7 OR X = 11 THEN 190
130   IF X<4 OR X>11 THEN 220
140   PRINT : PRINT
150   PRINT "YOUR POINT IS     ";X
160   P = X
170   F = 1 : PRINT : PRINT
180   GOTO 70
190   PRINT "NATURAL—YOU WIN!"
200   W = W + 1
210   GOTO 240
220   PRINT "CRAPS—YOU LOSE!"
230   L1 = L1 + 1
240   INPUT "ANOTHER ROLL?",Q$
250   IF Q$ # "N" THEN 60
260   PRINT "WINS = ";W
270   PRINT : PRINT "LOSSES = ";L1
280   PRINT : PRINT "TOTAL PLAYS = ";W+L1
290   END
300   IF X = 7 THEN 220
310   IF X = P THEN 190
320   GOTO 70
```

The Flag (F) is set when a condition occurs. The Flag is initialized to zero in line 60. Line 70 sets the roll of one die to A and line 80 sets the roll of the other die to B. RND(6) gives numbers from 0 to 5. Since die go from 1 to 6, a 1 must be added to RND to be in the proper range. Thus, RND(6) + 1 gives a range from 1 to 6. Line 90 sets the roll of both dice to X, and line 100 prints out the total score of the roll of the dice.

In line 110, the statement IF F = 1 THEN 300, causes the program to branch to line 300 to set up the condition to roll until a point is made, or until a 7 is rolled. Since F = 0 (line 60), the program defaults to line 120 to see if 7 or 11 has been rolled. Line 130 checks to see if a number below 4 or a number over 11 has been rolled. If neither a Win nor a Loss has been rolled, line 150 prints out, "YOUR POINT IS ___." (Note: the number given on line 100, is the value shown by the dashed line; for example, an 8.) Line 160 is a replacement statement that places the roll of the dice as your point ($P = X$). Line 170 sets the F (Flag) = 1. This is the condition that is used as a test to determine if the point has been made. The GOTO 70 statement on line 180 causes the dice to be rolled again. Since F = 1, line 110 branches to line 300. If the roll is 7 (with F = 1), the program branches to line 220 to inform you of your loss. If $X = P$ (Flag = 1), the program branches to line 190 to inform you of your win. If neither line 300 or line 310 is executed, the program defaults to line 320, where the GOTO 70 statement causes another roll of the dice.

After a win or a loss, the program defaults to the statement of line 240, INPUT "ANOTHER ROLL?",Q$ and, then, to line 250 and its statement of IF Q$ # "N" THEN 60. If you wish to roll again, press RETURN. If you wish to count your gains and losses, input "N" and press RETURN.

You might wonder why END is not at the end of the program. END can be placed anywhere in the program so long as it is accessed properly. The subroutines are placed after END in order to separate the body of the program from the subroutines. In this case, however, the statements were placed after the END as an example.

Five Card Stud

FIVE CARD STUD is a fascinating game of chance. In this program, the cards are shuffled, cut, and four hands of five cards are dealt. The program was written in a simple manner and, thus, just deals the hands. For a more complex program, the players could discard cards and draw new cards. Other variations could be included so as to determine the winner "according to Hoyle."

Games present many situations on which the programmer can practice his art. The following list contains some of the variables used in FIVE CARD STUD.

C = number of card where deck is cut.
D = deck of cards.
F$ = face cards.
J = loop variable.
K = loop variable to place 5 cards in a hand.
S = loop variable to shuffle card deck 5 times.
S$ = suit.

```
190  REM*FIVE CARD STUD
200  DIM D(52), S$(4), F$(4), Q$(1) : S = 5 : S$ = "SHCD" : F$ = "JQKA"
210  FOR J = 1 TO 52 : D(J) = J − 1 : NEXT J
220  FOR K = 1 TO S
```

```
230    FOR J = 52 TO 2 STEP −1
240    R = RND(J) + 1 : C = D(R) : D(R) = D(J) : D(J) = C : NEXT J,K
250    CALL −936 : C = RND(50) + 2 : PRINT "THIS DECK IS CUT AT CARD
       # ";C : PRINT
260    PRINT "PLYR #1  PLYR #2  PLYR #3  PLYR #4"
270    PRINT : FOR J = 1 TO 20
280    TAB(((J−1) MOD 4) + 1) *9 − 3
290    K = D(C) MOD 13
300    IF K>8 THEN PRINT F$(K−8,K−8); : IF K<9 THEN PRINT K + 2;
310    PRINT S$(D(C)/13 + 1, D(C)/13 + 1);
320    C = C + 1 : IF C = 53 THEN C = 1
330    IF J MOD 4 = 0 THEN PRINT
340    NEXT J : PRINT : PRINT
350    INPUT "ENTER 'E' TO END",Q$ : IF Q$ = "E" THEN 370
360    PRINT : INPUT "DO YOU WANT A NEW DECK? (Y OR N)",Q$ : IF Q$ =
       "Y" THEN 210 : GOTO 220
370    END
```

Line 200 DIMensions the limits in the deck, the suits, the face cards, and Q$ (for Y or N). It also initializes the variable S to 5 (the number of times the deck is shuffled), assigns the suit variables to the S$ (= "SHCD"), and assigns the face cards to the F$ (= "JQKA").

The line 210 statement of FOR J = 1 TO 52 : D(J) = J − 1 : NEXT J is a loop that places the deck of cards in memory using subscripted variables. The cards are placed in memory from 0 to 51 (J − 1), to facilitate truncation when the cards are divided into suits of 13 cards each.

Lines 220 through 240 are a unit of the program that is necessary in order to shuffle the cards 5 times: for K = 1 TO S (S = 5). The statement FOR J = 52 TO 1 STEP −1 shuffles the cards in reverse order. The R = RND(J) + 1 statement on line 240 places the cards in random order and then exchanges the cards through the statements C = D(R) : D(R) = D(J) : D(J) = C (also, on line 240). The nested loops are completed with the remaining statement of NEXT J,K.

Line 250 clears the screen (CALL −936), cuts the cards (C = RND(50) + 2), and prints out the heading, "THE DECK IS CUT AT CARD # ". The statement of line 260 properly spaces and prints out the headings for players 1 through 4.

Line 270 statement is PRINT; it skips a line and sets the subroutine FOR J = 1 TO 20 to outputting the 20 cards in the 4 hands—beginning at the number of the card where the cards were cut. The next 20 cards after the cut card comprise the 4 hands of 5 cards each.

Line 280 TAB(((J−1) MOD 4) + 1) *9 − 3 sets the TAB to print out the 5 cards present in each hand. The cards will be printed out in 4 rows with 9 spaces between each row, as shown in Table 20-1.

The line 300 statement is IF K>8 THEN PRINT F$(K−8,K−8);.

Table 20-1. Table of TAB Functions Used To Print Out Four Hands of Five Cards

HAND	CARD	J	TAB(((J−1) MOD 4) + 1)∗9 −3
1 (6)	1st	1	1-1 MOD 4 = 0+1 = 1∗9 = 9−3 = 6
2 (15)	1st	2	2-1 MOD 4 = 1+1 = 2∗9 = 18−3 = 15
3 (24)	1st	3	3-1 MOD 4 = 2+1 = 3∗9 = 27−3 = 24
4 (33)	1st	4	4-1 MOD 4 = 3+1 = 4∗9 = 36−3 = 33
1 (6)	2nd	5	5-1 MOD 4 = 0+1 = 1∗9 = 9−3 = 6
2 (15)	2nd	6	6-1 MOD 4 = 1+1 = 2∗9 = 18−3 = 15
3 (24)	2nd	7	7-1 MOD 4 = 2+1 = 3∗9 = 27−3 = 24
4 (33)	2nd	8	8-1 MOD 4 = 3+1 = 4∗9 = 36−3 = 33
1 (6)	3rd	9	9-1 MOD 4 = 0+1 = 1∗9 = 9−3 = 6
2 (15)	3rd	10	10-1 MOD 4 = 1+1 = 2∗9 = 18−3 = 15
3 (24)	3rd	11	11-1 MOD 4 = 2+1 = 3∗9 = 27−3 = 24
4 (33)	3rd	12	12-1 MOD 4 = 3+1 = 4∗9 = 36−3 = 33
1 (6)	4th	13	13-1 MOD 4 = 0+1 = 1∗9 = 9−3 = 6
2 (15)	4th	14	14-1 MOD 4 = 1+1 = 2∗9 = 18−3 = 15
3 (24)	4th	15	15-1 MOD 4 = 2+1 = 3∗9 = 27−3 = 24
4 (33)	4th	16	16-1 MOD 4 = 3+1 = 4∗9 = 36−3 = 33
1 (6)	5th	17	17-1 MOD 4 = 0+1 = 1∗9 = 9−3 = 6
2 (15)	5th	18	18-1 MOD 4 = 1+1 = 2∗9 = 18−3 = 15
3 (24)	5th	19	19-1 MOD 4 = 2+1 = 3∗9 = 27−3 = 24
4 (33)	5th	20	20-1 MOD 4 = 3+1 = 4∗9 = 36−3 = 33

If the value of the card is greater than 8 (the card values range from 0 to 8), any card after 8 will be a face card whose position is at memory location K−8,K−8. The second part of line 300 statement is IF K<9 THEN PRINT K + 2. If the value of the card is less than 9, print the value plus 2. This brings the range of numbered cards from 0 to 8 up to values of 2 to 10 (K + 2).

The line 310 statement of PRINT S$(D(C)/13 + 1, D(C)/13 + 1) is used to print out the suit of the card on the monitor screen next to the value of the card.

The statement on line 320 of C = C + 1 keeps tracks of from where the cards should be dealt to each of the players. The remainder of line 320 is the decision statement IF C = 53 THEN C = 1. The decision statement restarts the cards at number 1 when the fifty-second card has been dealt. The deal is started from the card number of the cut. If the cut is at card number 40, the first card dealt is card number 40.

The IF J MOD 4 = 0 THEN PRINT statement on line 330 closes out the line after the fourth printout, so that only four hands will be dealt to the players.

The line 340 statement of NEXT J is the end of the loop and PRINT : PRINT causes a skip of 2 lines before the line 350 statement of INPUT "ENTER 'E' TO END" ,Q$: IF Q$ = "E" THEN 370 causes the program to END if "E" is input. If RETURN is pressed, another series of hands is dealt.

Line 360 statement is a question; PRINT : INPUT "DO YOU WANT A NEW DECK? (Y OR N)", Q$. If "Y" (yes) is input, the program branches to line 210 to select a new deck, shuffle the deck, and cut the cards. If "N" (no) is input, the program branches to line 220 to shuffle the remaining cards of the old deck.

EXERCISE

Define ten new words from your computer dictionary.

Appendix

This book was written so that most of the lessons and programs were completely explained within the lesson section, itself. However, not all the details of programming can be presented in one book. The programs that are used were developed so that the student could improvise and create programs more suitable to his or her specific needs. However, the programs in this appendix seemed necessary to augment the learning experience gained from Lessons 14, 15, and 16.

FURTHER EXPLANATION OF SORT PROGRAMS

Lesson 14 was a lesson in MIN-MAX and SORT programs. The Comparison of 3 Sorts program that follows is derived from three sources: (1) Lines 200 to 250 were learned at a major American university, (2) Lines 310 to 370 were learned from public sources and are used in business, and (3) Lines 410 through 470 is a SORT developed independently by the author.

There are many sorts available but the three sorts in the following program are simple and effective when used for less than 200 items in a list. The variables used in the Comparison of 3 Sorts program are:

L—is an array with a standard data set so that when each sort is tested, it can be compared with a standard data set without destroying the original data set.

S—array to be sorted.

T$—holds the printout of the order of the array to be sorted. The program contains three nested loops that determine:

1. Which type of sort is to be used.
   A. Bubble sort.
   B. Random sort.

C. Greatest-to-least sort.
2. Which case is to be used in the sort.
 A. First array—least to greatest order.
 B. Second array—random order.
 C. Third array—greatest to least order.
3. Number of items to be sorted.
 A. 50 to 200 with following steps.
  (1) 50
  (2) 100
  (3) 150
  (4) 200

I—loop indicator that controls the number of items to be sorted.
R$—pause (dummy) variable.
M—loop variable.
N—loop variable.

```
90   REM*COMPARISON OF 3 SORTS
100  DIM L(200), S(200), T$(20)
110  FOR J = 1 TO 200 : L(J) = RND(100) : NEXT J
120  FOR K = 1 TO 3 : FOR V = 50 TO 200 STEP 50 : FOR J = 1 TO 3
130  GOSUB 500 : GOTO J*10 + 130
140  GOSUB 200 : GOTO 170
150  GOSUB 300 : GOTO 170
160  GOSUB 400
170  NEXT J,V,K
199  END
200  PRINT "BUBBLE SORT : CASE";T$ : PRINT "NUMBER OF ITEMS = ";V :
     INPUT R$
210  FOR M = 1 TO V − 1 : F = 1
220  FOR N = 1 TO V − M
230  IF S(N) < = S(N+1) THEN 250
240  F = 0 : W = S(N) : S(N) = S(N+1) : S(N+1) = W
250  NEXT N : IF F THEN 260 : NEXT M
260  PRINT "SORT COMPLETED!!!" : INPUT R$ : RETURN
300  PRINT "EXCHANGE SORT : CASE"; T$ : PRINT "NUMBER OF ITEMS =
     ";V : INPUT R$
310  FOR M = 1 TO V − 1
320  FOR N = M + 1 TO V
330  IF S(M) <= S(N) THEN 350
340  W = S(M) : S(M) = S(N) : S(N) = W
350  NEXT N : IF M MOD 5 # 0 THEN 370
360  FOR W = M TO V − 1 : IF S(W)>S(W+1) THEN 370 : NEXT W : GOTO
     380
370  NEXT M
380  PRINT "SORT COMPLETED!!!" : INPUT R$ : RETURN
400  PRINT "MIN-MAX SORT : CASE";T$ : PRINT "NUMBER OF ITEMS = ";V :
     INPUT R$
410  FOR N = 1 TO V − 1 : W = N
420  FOR M = N + 1 TO V
430  IF S(M) <= S(W) THEN W = M
440  NEXT M : M = S(N) : S(N) = S(W) : S(W) = M
450  IF N MOD 5 # 0 THEN 470
```

```
460   FOR M = N TO V − 1 : IF S(M)>S(M+1) THEN 470 : NEXT M : GOTO
      480
470   NEXT N
480   PRINT "SORT COMPLETED!!!" : INPUT R$ : RETURN
500   GOTO K∗10 + 500
510   FOR M = 1 TO V : S(M) = M : NEXT M : T$ = "LEAST TO GREATEST" :
      RETURN
520   FOR M = 1 TO V : S(M) = L(M) : NEXT M : T$ = "RANDOM ORDER" :
      RETURN
530   FOR M = 1 TO V : S(M) = V − M : NEXT M : T$ = "GREATEST TO
      LEAST" : RETURN
RUN
BUBBLE SORT : CASE LEAST TO GREATEST
            : CASE RANDOM ORDER
            : CASE GREATEST TO LEAST
NUMBER OF ITEMS = (50 to 200)
  (PRESS RETURN — R$ IN PROGRAM)
SORT COMPLETED!!!
  (PRESS RETURN)
EXCHANGE SORT : CASE LEAST TO GREATEST
              : CASE RANDOM ORDER
              : CASE GREATEST TO LEAST
NUMBER OF ITEMS = (50 to 200)
  (PRESS RETURN)
SORT COMPLETED!!!
  (PRESS RETURN)
MIN-MAX SORT : CASE LEAST TO GREATEST
             : CASE RANDOM ORDER
             : CASE GREATEST TO LEAST
NUMBER OF ITEMS = (50 to 200)
  (PRESS RETURN)
SORT COMPLETED!!!
```

ADDITIONAL FLOWCHARTING INFORMATION

Lesson 15 is supplemented in this section by a flowchart that contains a loop. This loop is used to check that there are exactly two delimiters in the Name and Address program input. The Name and Address program used in Lesson 15 checked the delimiters at the end of each field. The flowchart shown in Fig. A-1 checks the delimiters at the input.

Lesson 15 is also supplemented with a detailed explanation of a method to compare strings. Since strings cannot be compared by an IF   THEN statement (direct comparison), it is necessary to determine which string is shorter. The shortest string is printed first. If the strings are equal in length, the computer must compare the characters in each position, i.e., the first character to the last character, if necessary. When two nonequal characters are found, the character with the least ASCII (American Standard Code for Information Interchange) code will determine which string is printed first. The list given in Table A-1 is a partial listing of the ASCII code numbers for a space and the alpha characters.

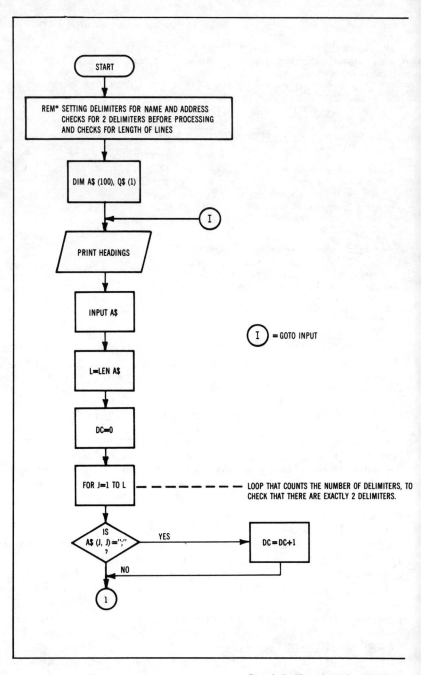

Fig. A-1. Flowchart for checking

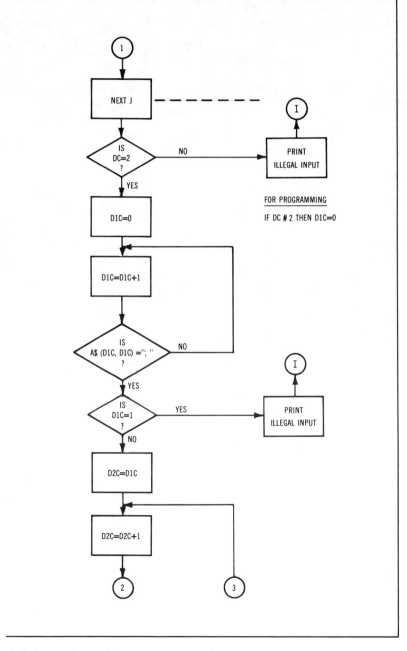

delimiters at input of program.

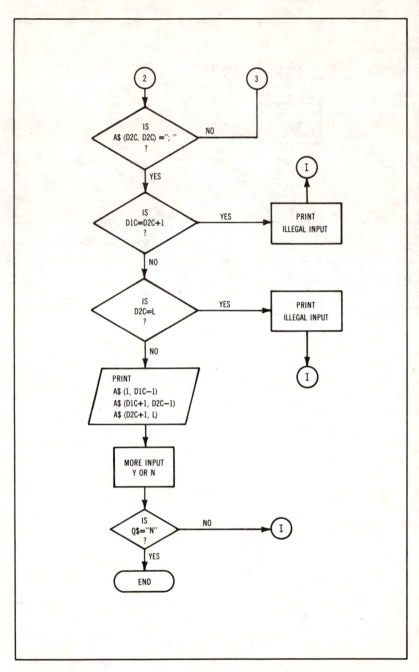

Fig. A-1. Cont. Flowchart for checking delimiters at input of program.

Table A-1. ASCII Character Coding

Space	160	A	193	B	194	C	195
D	196	E	197	F	198	G	199
H	200	I	201	J	202	K	203
L	204	M	205	N	206	O	207
P	208	Q	209	R	210	S	211
T	212	U	213	V	214	W	215
X	216	Y	217	Z	218		

Some of the variables that are used in the Compare Strings program are:

AL—length of A$.
BL—Length of B$.
CL—common length.

```
90    REM*COMPARE STRINGS
100   DIM A$(20), B$(20)
110   INPUT A$ : INPUT B$
120   AL = LEN(A$) : BL = LEN(B$)
130   CL = AL : IF BL<AL THEN CL = BL
140   FOR J = 1 TO CL
145   PRINT A$(J,J);" = ";ASC(A$(J,J)),B$(J,J); " = " ; ASC(B$(J,J))
150   IF ASC(A$(J,J))<ASC(B$(J,J)) THEN 190
160   IF ASC(A$(J,J))<ASC(B$(J,J)) THEN 210
170   NEXT J
180   IF AL<BL THEN GOSUB 250 : IF BL<AL THEN GOSUB 270 : IF AL = BL
      THEN GOSUB 290 : GOTO 249
190   GOSUB 250 : GOTO 249
210   GOSUB 270
249   END
250   PRINT A$ : PRINT B$ : RETURN
270   PRINT B$ : PRINT A$ : RETURN
290   PRINT A$ : RETURN
RUN
SMYTH
SMITH
S = 211      S = 211
M = 205      M = 205
Y = 217      I = 201
SMITH
SMYTH
RUN
ABCX
ABCD
A = 193      A = 193
B = 194      B = 194
C = 195      C = 195
X = 216      D = 196
ABCD
ABCX
```

```
RUN
BELL
BEAL
B  =  194      B  =  194
E  =  197      E  =  197
L  =  204      A  =  193
BEAL
BELL
```

MORE GRAPHICS DISPLAYS

The following GRaphics augmentation of Lesson 16 is a Christmas present for you. The first program is for use on a black and white tv screen and produces a Christmas tree picture.

```
2     REM*CHRISTMAS TREE
5     CALL −936
10    VTAB 6
20    FOR X = 1 TO 15
30    TAB 21 − X
40    FOR T = 1 TO (X*2) − 1
50    PRINT "*" ;
60    NEXT T
70    PRINT
80    NEXT X
90    FOR Z = 1 TO 4
100   TAB 18
110   PRINT "*****"
120   NEXT Z
130   END
```

The final program is a Christmas tree design for use with a color tv. It outputs a beautiful green Christmas tree with a base. The program pauses and, then, states: "SOMEBODY PLUG IN THE LIGHTS!". The lights are turned on, and they blink randomly, in different colors, all over the tree. A blinking varicolored star sits atop the tree, and underneath the tree is the caption, "M E R R Y C H R I S T M A S !". This is a beautiful program for use at Christmas time. It will stay on the tv screen until any key is pressed. The variables for the Christmas Tree With Lights program are:

SQX—holds the X value of a specific square.
SQY—holds the Y value of a specific square.
FLAG—a flag for a condition that is to be tested. There are 16 flags; one for each of the light-string conditions that must be tested for an on (1) or an off (0).
LTCOL—an array that holds the various colors of the lights.
J—a loop variable.
X—the value on the screen used to develop the positions of the lights.

Y—the value on the screen used to develop the position of the lights.

M—the number that determines which light set is to be turned on (1) or off (0).

N—the loop variable used to turn on or off the last four lights in each set.

```
1    CALL -936 : REM*CHRISTMAS TREE WITH LIGHTS
5    GOTO 90
9    REM*LINES 10 - 80 SETS UP THE POSITION OF THE TREE LIGHTS AND
     THEIR COLORS
10   DIM SQX(75), SQY(75), FLAG(75), LTCOL(6)
15   LTCOL(0) = 1 : LTCOL(1) = 3 : LTCOL(2) = 7
20   LTCOL(3) = 9 : LTCOL(4) = 11 : LTCOL(5) = 13
25   LTCOL(6) = 8
30   FOR J = 0 TO 75 : FLAG(J) = 0 : SQX(J) = 0 : SQY(J) = 0 : NEXT J
35   FOR J = 0 TO 75
40   Y = RND(32) + 5 : L = (Y-2)/2
45   X = 19 - L + RND(2*L + 1)
50   FOR L = 0 TO J
55   IF SQX(L) = X AND SQY(L) = Y THEN 40
60   NEXT L
65   SQX(J) = X : SQY(J) = Y
70   NEXT J
80   GOTO 201
85   REM*LINES 90 TO 200 DRAW THE TREE THEN GOTO 10 TO STRING THE
     LIGHTS
90   GR
100  COLOR = 0
111  FOR I = 0 TO 39
112  VLIN 0, 39 AT I
113  NEXT I
115  COLOR = 4
120  FOR I = 3 TO 36
160  L = (I-2)/2
170  HLIN 19 - L, 19 + L AT I
180  NEXT I
185  COLOR = 8
190  FOR I = 37 TO 39
200  HLIN 17,21 AT I : NEXT I : PRINT "SOMEBODY PLUG IN THE LIGHTS!" :
     GOTO 10
201  VTAB 23 : PRINT "THERE WE GO" : FOR L = 1 TO 900 : NEXT L :
     PRINT : PRINT : PRINT
202  TAB 16 : PRINT "M E R R Y"
203  TAB 13 : PRINT "C H R I S T M A S"
204  PRINT : REM*THESE THREE LOOPS MAKE THE TREE STAY LIT FOR A
     LONG TIME
205  FOR L = 0 TO 100
210  FOR J = 0 TO 100
215  REM*LINES 220 TO 360 ILLUMINATE THE STAR
220  FOR I = 1 TO 4
230  GOTO I*10 + 230
240  COLOR = 1 : GOTO 300
250  COLOR = 2 : GOTO 300
```

```
260   COLOR = 9 : GOTO 300
270   COLOR = 11 : GOTO 300
280   COLOR = 13
300   GOTO ((I+J−1) MOD 5)*10 + 310
310   PLOT 18,3 : PLOT 17,3 : GOTO 360
320   PLOT 18,2 : PLOT 17,1 : GOTO 360
330   PLOT 19,2 : PLOT 19,1 : PLOT 19,0 : GOTO 360
340   PLOT 20,2 : PLOT 21,1 : GOTO 360
350   PLOT 20,3 : PLOT 21,3
360   NEXT I
361   REM*LINES 363 TO 450 TURN THE LIGHTS ON OR OFF RANDOMLY :
      THERE ARE 15 SETS OF 5 LIGHTS EACH AND 1 INDIVIDUAL LIGHT
362   REM*IF THE SELECTED SET IS OFF THEN IT IS TURNED ON. IF THE SELECTED
      SET IS ON THEN IT IS TURNED OFF.
363   FOR N = 1 TO 25
365   M = RND (76)
370   IF FLAG(M) THEN 420
380   C = RND(7) : COLOR = LTCOL(C)
390   PLOT SQX(M), SQY(M) : FLAG(M) = 1
400   GOTO 450
420   FLAG(M) = 0
430   COLOR = 4
440   PLOT SQX(M), SQY(M)
450   FOR I = 0 TO 15 : NEXT I, N, J, L
500   TEXT : CALL −936 : END
```

Index

TO THE READER

Sams Computer books cover Fundamentals — Programming — Interfacing — Technology written to meet the needs of computer engineers, professionals, scientists, technicians, students, educators, business owners, personal computerists and home hobbyists.

Our Tradition is to meet your needs
and in so doing we invite you to tell us what
your needs and interests are by completing
the following:

1. I need books on the following topics:

_____

_____

_____

_____

_____

_____

2. I have the following Sams titles:

_____

_____

_____

_____

_____

_____

3. My occupation is:

_____ Scientist, Engineer   _____ D P Professional

_____ Personal computerist   _____ Business owner

_____ Technician, Serviceman   _____ Computer store owner

_____ Educator   _____ Home hobbyist

_____ Student   Other _____

_____

Name (print) _____

Address _____

City _____ State _____ Zip _____

Mail to: **Howard W. Sams & Co., Inc.**
Marketing Dept. #CBS1/80
4300 W. 62nd St., P.O. Box 7092
Indianapolis, Indiana 46206

21812